HUSSEIN

ART of
RESILIENCE

The REFUGEE STATE of MIND

LIONCREST
PUBLISHING

ART OF RESILIENCE

The Refugee State of Mind

ISBN   978-1-5445-2150-3 *Hardcover*
       978-1-5445-2149-7 *Paperback*
       978-1-5445-2148-0 *Ebook*

To the sun and the moon of my universe, my mother and father.

CONTENTS

———

FOREWORD

JEVON MCCORMICK, PRESIDENT AND CEO, SCRIBE MEDIA

WHEN I FIRST MET HUSSEIN EARLY ON IN HIS JOURney writing the book you're now reading, we connected immediately. We both come from backgrounds filled with challenges for which we're grateful. We both have personal experience in uncovering our gifts and talents through discipline, patience, and practice. We both believe in the power of our state of mind, which is a choice we make every day. And through our experiences speaking to audiences of all ages and backgrounds, we've both learned that everyone has a story and that you can make a powerful impact just by telling yours.

Like Hussein, I often tell my story in front of large audiences. It can be scary making yourself that vulnerable to a crowd of unfamiliar faces. When I first began sharing my story on stage, and especially when I published my book, *I Got There*, I wondered if anyone would care. Would they understand where I was coming from? Would they see me differently? How would they react to my story?

What happened once I began sharing it was truly unexpected. Each time I stepped off the stage, people came up to me with one particular goal. They approached me to thank me for telling my story. And then they shared theirs with me.

They said, "I've never told anyone my story before. I see why it's important now."

Hussein's story, like mine, is one of survival. More than that, Hussein's story is one of resilience defined by peeling back the layers of his story and heritage. By telling his story, Hussein shows us that purpose is the gold that your internal guiding compass is made from. Purpose leads us to meaningful work for ourselves, the community, and the world. Hussein paints a picture of a journey to a higher state of mind uncovered through deep reflection and gratitude for his past experiences.

The story you are about to read opened my eyes a little wider to understanding my own power and resilience. I believe it will do the same for you.

PREFACE

—

I DISCOVERED THE POWER OF SHARING MY STORY when a young man named Oscar came up to me in a cadet uniform. Hannah, my wife, and I were selling screen-printed T-shirts out of our 1985 Volkswagen van at a local night market outside of Portland, Oregon. It was the early days of Refutees, my business designing social cause merchandise to raise awareness for refugees.

"You don't remember me," the young man said, "but you spoke at my school a few years ago about your story."

"You remember me from that long ago?" I asked. I was genuinely surprised. A friend of mine, a teacher at a middle school, had asked me to come to share my journey with his class. I gave a short talk about my life experience when I was their age: how life in America was different for me and how I studied architecture in college and started a T-shirt printing company.

"You changed my life," Oscar said. "I was failing classes and blamed everyone else. That day, I went home and started doing chores and doing my homework. I didn't want to be a dropout. I wanted to make my mom proud of me."

I started to tear up. I looked over at Hannah. She was listening and tearing up, too. I never knew how much impact my journey could have on others.

"I turned my grades around, started helping around the house, and changed my attitude. I was able to graduate and join the police academy. I hope to be a detective one day and help people."

At this point, I was full-blown crying. "All that from a talk at school?" I asked, staring deep into his eyes.

"It was how you made me believe that I'm no different than you," he said. Though he was from the suburbs of Portland, Oregon, and I spent my early years in Iraq and a refugee camp in Saudi Arabia, we had more in common than not. We shared the immigrant experience of having to come to a different land and learn, adapt, and feel pressured to form ourselves in uncomfortable ways.

I hugged him tight and told him to stay in touch and gave him some T-shirts. I felt a sense of service I had never felt before, and I couldn't stop talking about the moment for weeks. It was humbling to realize I had actually made an impact.

His story solidified the power of my voice; I knew I was onto something. Through the years of sharing my story at schools, networking events, and leadership conferences, it became clear I could help educators, students, and leaders feel inspired and empowered. My own experience would be an example for others on how to tap into their innate layers of resilience.

The process of telling my story has helped me unpack my story in a way that was deep and therapeutic. I dug through layers of time and space that shaped my journey—both the joyful moments and the traumas. I think of my past as an energy source to move me forward. I call this ability, to transform pain into power, having a "Refugee State of Mind."

No matter where we were born, all of our ancestors have been travelers, seekers of better opportunities, and gatherers of knowledge. A sense of curiosity, a thirst for adventure, and, most importantly, a desire to find our true calling is what makes us human.

This book is not about the statistics of the refugee crisis, or how we can save all refugees and end all wars. I don't have clear solutions for the wrongs that have taken place and continue to transpire around the world. I can only tell one story, my story.

INTRODUCTION

———

*My family and I were huddled in the corner of my parents'
room, waiting for the inevitable—missiles aimed at our
city of As-Samawah, southeast of Baghdad, Iraq.*

*That night, the sky was raining missiles, bombing bridges,
armories, and communication towers. Those that missed
their targets headed straight for schools, businesses, and
civilian homes.*

*I felt the squeeze of my father's arms wrapping my whole
family. The bombs were getting closer and louder. Each
blast was scarier than the last. My father started praying
in a low whisper. "Thank you, Allah, for what you have
given me."*

*His eyes filled up with tears, and I could hear surrender
in his voice. He began to repeat the "Al-Fatiha" prayer, the*

opening verse from the first chapter of the Quran, and my
mother and my six siblings joined in. "If we die in this
moment, may Allah forgive us and grant us paradise."

I pause my speech and take a moment to scan the audi-
torium full of hundreds of people. I had been asked to
speak at an awards ceremony for outstanding educators,
administrators, community leaders, and support staff of
local K-12 schools.

The audience is silent, hanging on to my every word, while
watching pictures from my past fill the giant screens
behind me. I share my story of how my father's art saved
our lives at the refugee camp. How art has continually
shaped my life through difficult times. I have relied on
improving my artistic abilities to get me through college
and build my business. Using art in different forms has
helped me cope, become flexible, optimistic, and most of
all, build the layers of resilience for my journey.

I tell the audience how my family was spared that horrible
night, but our lives changed forever. We fled to a refugee
camp in Saudi Arabia and finally made it to America. I
share more stories of resilience, the important lessons
I've learned along the way, and how making art became a
source of healing. I give a shoutout to the teachers that had
the most impact on me, helping me build my perspective
and hone my passion.

As I walk off the stage to loud applause, I notice my anxiety and fears have transformed into a feeling of utter calm. I feel vulnerable, but full of courage, like I was supposed to be on that stage, at this very night and moment to tell this specific story. I feel a sense of purpose realized. I am no longer voiceless, rather a composed artistic expression of a message sent to the future from that refugee camp I once roamed.

My calm comes from the strength I have long built over the years. Facing challenges has given me an edge over my nerves. Growth happens when we get uncomfortable. Once we move forward, we will stumble. This is part of the process. We're all on a journey towards greater self-discovery. Challenges are unavoidable, but it's how we build layers of resilience to face those challenges that defines our lives.

The layers of resilience I write about are not ones I have invented for the purposes of this book. I have continually spent time reading about the self, personal growth, and how to learn to heal, trying to understand why my behaviors and actions are triggered by past trauma I never knew I had. Trauma that is deeply buried in stories, shame, blame, neglect of physical and mental health, and seeking approval. My survivor's guilt was deep, and I needed a way to learn to cope. Learning to name and understand my deep emotional states helped me further understand who and what I am.

Uncovering the stories that transformed my pain into power became a way to study myself. I wanted to create a state of mind that I can always rely on throughout life. I used to be very embarrassed that I came from a refugee camp, poverty, and welfare. This was the shame that I needed to turn inside out. Embracing these stories, owning them, comfortably speaking about them was the essence of my state of mind. The Refugee State of Mind.

In the following pages, I will unpack the layers of resilience that have gotten me to where I am.

From stomping mud in a pit to make bricks to use as shelter to getting into the architecture program at Portland State University, I met challenges at every stage of growth—like when I sold Portland T-shirts and got fined by the NBA. From watching my father paint in the refugee camp to becoming an artist and painting my heart out at poetry nights to pay my way through college. From fist fights after 9/11 to realizing that the ink of a scholar is worth more than blood spilled over anger. From being and feeling voiceless to turning up the microphones while I shared my story to thousands of students, teachers, and leaders.

Through these layers, I found myself. I came across opportunities to travel, speak, paint murals, form unbreakable bonds, and earn money doing what I loved. I found my wife, or maybe she found me—either way it wouldn't have happened had I not started a Hookah business venture that failed. I walked away with something more amazing—a supportive, loving companion on my journey. So much of what I wanted to work out didn't, and I came to realize that's OK, too. What's meant for me will or has come.

It was my job to be aware and live in a state of gratitude while I sought better versions of myself, allowing my deep inner guiding compass to build my mission and support me through my journey. I can't control life and how it unfolds, but learning to rely on my resilience is the key to getting through just about anything.

These stories are from experiences that I call layers, which built a beautiful pattern of tenacity. I hope you can reflect on your own mishaps and see what you have learned from them. When you face an uncomfortable or difficult situation, you can use a layer, or multiple layers, to help you through it. Something about your true calling may reveal itself to you. You may find a mission or a new life awaiting you.

When hearing my story, I hope you will come to recognize and define your own resilience—the mental fortitude that leads to inner peace. Through reflecting on your experiences, you will realize you have survived and have made it through tough times, too. Reflecting is asking your past self questions to understand your state of mind. Revisiting stories of joy and challenges and coming to a resolution is essential to personal growth. What stories do you tell yourself? How can you tell yourself a new positive perspective on that story?

Your triumph over the smallest battle is crucial. There's no such thing as failing. You can learn from past experiences, change, and shapeshift your attitude to a positive one. Here is where you can earn that new state of mind. Name it, own it, and allow it to drive your actions and positive thoughts of the future you want to create.

From this practice of reflection, you will learn to develop, trust, and embrace what you have long struggled with and turn into your own power source: your state of mind.

LAYER 1

HOPE IN THE RUBBLE

"MOMMA, WILL DAD COME BACK TONIGHT?"

With tears coming down her cheeks, she replied, "Yes, Inshallah Habibi."

"Momma, what does Inshallah mean?"

"It means, 'If God wills it to be,'" she said, hugging my siblings and me.

It has taken me decades to understand the word "Inshallah" entirely—a deep inner knowing that hope comes from a belief. If you sincerely believe something is, it will be. You leave life not to chance, but rather a deep knowing that it will all work out according to a higher plan. In other words, what you think expands.

Hope doesn't appear in the form of a particular figure reaching into the rubble to pull you out of the darkness. It's an elusive feeling tucked deep inside yourself, nudging you forward through difficult times. It's a prayer, it's a split-second decision. Even when the odds are against us, we desire things to work out. Desire needs an energy source to tap into; this is where our beliefs come into play.

It's difficult to point to the exact moment when hope comes to save you from the darkness. Hope speaks through a subtle voice, only known to you.

Hope is the first, deepest layer of resilience. It is the moment of tension between deep knowing and uncertainty. Hope is a match lit in the darkest of corners, lighting up the room. Our beliefs are the fuel, keeping the match lit.

UNDER A DARK CLOUD

———

AT FIVE YEARS OLD, I WATCHED FROM OUR FRONT door while I cracked it open to see what was happening outside as an old man tripped on the curb and landed face first in the gutter. He lay lifeless for a few moments and then picked himself up and wiped his face as he started running again.

My mom ran around the house and covered the windows with blankets. She shouted orders at my older siblings to stay low as they moved around the house. Emergency sirens blared, telling us to stay inside and get to safety. From outside, I could hear women and men shouting and crying for help.

Above my head, military jets ripped through the air. Suddenly, everything became silent. The sound was so loud it pierced my eardrums. All I could hear was a loud ringing noise. Another man ran past our house and fell flat on his face. He lay there, helpless and unconscious. He wore a traditional dishdasha, a long white robe usually worn by men in the Middle East, with a red and white scarf—the traditional kaffiyeh—atop his head. His white dishdasha started to turn red up and down his back. My eyes widened and my heart started to beat faster. I wondered if he was ever going to get up again.

"They bombed the bridge, they bombed the bridge!" my mom screamed out, "Oh, Allah, please return my boys and husband to me!" She paced back and forth. I started coughing from the dust. The air smelled of burning oil, under a dark cloud from the burning oil refineries.

I had the urge to go out into the chaos to see if I could wake up the man on the street. While I held our front door open to watch him, two men ran up and carried his lifeless body away.

"Hussein! Hussein!" my mom called out. She ran up behind me, reached around my whole body, and pulled me away from the front door, slamming it behind her. She locked it tightly with a lever and rushed me to her bedroom, where some of my siblings were huddled together.

The bombing barrage continued for a few more hours. My mother held us all in the corner of her bedroom, where we waited in the darkness with a few candles. The ringing in my ears finally began to fade and my hearing was coming back to me, as I could make out her sniffles and cries. We didn't know where my older brothers and father were, and if they were still alive.

Suddenly, we heard a loud array of thuds and knocking on the door. The knocking kept getting louder and wouldn't stop. I felt my mother's tight hug get tighter. It could have been the US ground troops, ready to kill us. She got up and ran to the door, not knowing if death was on the other side.

"Open the door! It's me, Ali!"

My uncle, Ali, burst in and immediately locked the door behind him. He told us my brothers and father were safe. They were hiding out at my relative's house until it became a little safer to make it back.

My brothers and father finally made it back home later that evening. The bombings continued through the night. We all huddled in my parents' room in the corner. I heard my father's prayers and felt the trembling in my mom's cries. I felt my siblings shivering from fear and hugging me tighter as bombings got louder.

My father and even my brothers had spent years paying for our three-bedroom house on the outskirts of the city, and it was about to crumble to pieces. Everything was covered in dust, the walls cracked, the windows blown out by the vibrations of the jets ripping through the sky. The structure could fall apart on us while we huddled inside.

I suddenly opened my eyes as my mother nudged me awake. I watched everyone scramble around the house packing bags, getting ready for the bus that was coming to get us and people in our neighborhood to the Salt Mines on the border of Saudi Arabia. The sun was rising, no call to prayer today. I didn't have a bad dream; I was actually living this nightmare. I heard my mother and father shouting orders to hurry so we could get on the bus to get us out of the city.

My mother scooped me up, kissing me and hugging me and rushing me into the bathroom to wash me up and dress me, and she sat me down by the luggage. I was so confused. "Where are we going, Momma?" I asked.

"Hussein, we have to leave right away; it's not safe here now."

I heard my father tell her, "The Rebels are taking control of the cities. We'll come back if things get better, but for now we have to get out of here in case the bombings get worse tonight! We will be OK, Inshallah."

I saw my mother wipe her tears and pack food and essentials as quickly as she could. My father packed some belongings from his art studio; from his dresser, I saw him pack cash and his most prized possession, a gold watch he had won for his art a few years prior.

In these moments of utter chaos, my father kept saying "Inshallah" and "alhamdulillah"—thanking God that we survived last night's bombing barrage. Hope showed up when the sun came out.

POWER TO THE REBELS

IT WAS 1991 AND IRAQ, THE COUNTRY MY PARENTS knew and loved, had been in the dark ages for centuries. Baghdad, the capital, was once the biggest exporter of knowledge and once a central hub for all religions, ideas, and trade. Throughout the 1900s, Iraq's government was unstable, ruled by the British, who installed a monarchy which later was overthrown by tribes and military generals. Then came the worst one of all, taking power in 1979. General Saddam Hussein became an Iraqi dictator and held on to power with an iron fist. The rich art, theatre, and poetry scene of the '50s and '60s that my father had been a crucial part of was long over.

Saddam Hussein's ruthless tyranny had drained Iraq of its life. He kept all the wealth to the state and starved his people. His propaganda spread through all newspapers, television, radio. Much like Hitler had Nazis, Saddam had his Bath Party. They were everywhere, spying on citizens and reporting back to the government. This meant pretty much anything out of line would get you beaten up, put in jail, or even executed.

My family and I were among the many marginalized Shi'a Muslims in the south of Iraq. A few months before the bombing of our town, Saddam Hussein started what would be known as the Gulf War. On August 2, 1990, Saddam invaded the neighboring country of Kuwait and seized control within two days. The United States ordered Saddam Hussein to pull his troops out, but Saddam refused. In response, the United States and allied forces waged an air war against Iraq for six weeks. Oil refineries were on fire, and the black smoke filled the air. One after another, entire cities fell. Everything from military to civil infrastructure was under attack. The United States' campaign encountered little resistance from the Iraqi air force. The Iraqi ground forces were helpless and lost endless troops.

As the Iraqi troops surrendered and began pulling out of Kuwait, the US bombing barrage hit Iraqi troops the hardest. This was called the Highway of Death Air Strike, which annihilated Iraqi troops leaving Kuwait. Saddam's government and military lost their grip on national security. This created time and hope for a rebellion group to take back the country from Saddam Hussein. Rumors spread that the US military was helping rebel forces overthrow Saddam and free the Iraqi people. People in many southern cities of Iraq began to raid the armories in hopes of helping the Rebels free Iraq from the ruthless dictator. For the first time in over ten years, hope surfaced to try and take down the dictator.

As the wrath of Saddam unfolded, things went from bad to worse. The US Army retreated out of Iraq and aid to the Rebels diminished. Hope during these days turned to uncertainty and fear. Saddam began to send his troops to take back the cities that fell to rebels at whatever cost. He bombed his own people through the night. This was the day I looked out the door of my house and saw the chaos unfold on my neighborhood street. The night of the heavy bombing of our city was the night we survived, huddled in our parents' bedroom corner.

That very next morning we began to load onto a bus full of other families from our community. The driver wouldn't allow my older brothers to get on. Saddam's armies were at every checkpoint, tracking down young rebels. My father argued with the man. The bus driver told my brothers he would meet them about eight miles away at the farmer's bridge, after the checkpoint.

My brothers ran as fast as they could, through farmland and high grass, and hid around the checkpoints. They finally made it back to the bus, and we all arrived at the

Salt Mines, where hundreds of other families were gathered. Everyone was in a frenzy asking one another about the latest news updates.

A group of men, including some of my male relatives, decided to split off and walk to the border of Saudi Arabia. They did not want to bring more danger to families, women, and children. My dad decided it was time to send Alaa, my oldest brother, to go with this group of men seeking refuge, in case anyone came looking for him. My father gave him a list of his friends' names and phone numbers in Iran if he ended up there.

Alaa was a calligraffiti artist. He had learned the art of calligraphy at a very young age from working with my father in his small sign shop, making painted banners, posters, and signs for the community. A few weeks before, he had gathered the most vibrant paint he could find and painted the words "Power to the Rebels" on the wall of a nearby high school.

When the Rebels passed by the wall, they cheered and honked their horns. No one had so publicly made such a bold statement against the government in years. Calligraffiti was the ultimate form of self-expression. Though he felt a sense of pride, he was young and scared. Someone a few stories up, in an apartment building, had been watching him.

My mom gave him a rolled-up blanket and a small water cooler. They hugged while she tried to hold back her tears. Alaa went with the men and started the trek through the desert along the one road leading them to a safer place. My mother cried most of the evening, not knowing if we would see him again.

After a few days of living in the salt mine, our supplies and essentials were dwindling. My mother and father had to make yet another difficult decision to split up. My father knew that he and my older brother Yas would not be safe if they returned to our city. Men were being targeted and either jailed or murdered.

Word got back to the Salt Mines of a green zone that was a safe place to get to. Many men were there, and they were asking families to join, too. The men sent to report to people in the Salt Mines were our neighbors, and they assured my mother that Alaa and the other men had made it to safety. A group of men with a stolen fire truck picked the men up and brought them to the border, where the US military gave them water and food. My father and brother Yas set out for this safe zone, too.

Now it was up to my mom to take all the kids back to the city, grab some supplies, and try to meet up with my father and brothers on the other side of the border. The drive back was very scary as we saw fires in the distance and smoke filling the air around our city of Al-Samawah. The checkpoints were filled with Saddam's National Guard searching for young rebels. Our entire neighborhood was unrecognizable from the debris and crumbled buildings. When we finally made it home, it was a surprise that it was intact. We got dropped off and we rushed inside to grab supplies. My mother and siblings filled duffle bags and tote bags with canned food, cooking supplies, candles, clothes, and blankets. It was as much as we could carry with us to head to the unknown.

Saddam had started yet another military campaign, and our city was next to get picked through and raided. We needed to go before Saddam's armies arrived. A caravan of city trucks moved through the town, picking up anyone who needed a ride out. In the middle of the night, we all got on the bed of a crowded gravel carrier truck and said goodbye to our home. This time, there was no going back.

I fell asleep on my sister's lap, and when I woke up, the sun was rising. I peeked over the metal wall of the gravel trailer as we drove through the Safe Zone gates. There was a crowd of men and women waiting to reunite with their families.

I scanned the crowd back and forth, and finally, I saw a hand wave followed by a shout, "HUSSEIN! HUSSEIN!" I looked out and saw my father. When I saw him and locked eyes, he smiled so big, and his eyes filled up with tears of joy.

I pointed to him and called out, "Momma, there he is!" We all got out of the trailer, and we hugged and kissed each other with a sigh of relief that we were once again reunited.

There were makeshift tents everywhere and people scattered for as far as my eyes could see. Dad walked us to where Alaa, Yas, and he had been sleeping the past few days underneath a familiar red and brown blanket that they had pitched up like a small tent. I ran up and threw myself at them and squeezed and hugged them.

It was official. We were refugees, seeking safety in an unknown land.

LAYER 2

SUPPORTIVE STRUCTURES

IT'S DIFFICULT TO IMAGINE WHERE I WOULD BE without my family and the supportive environment they created for me as a young boy. What does it mean to have support? I learned that a home could be as simple as a tent, but the love that resides there is the structure that sustains the life within.

The structures around you, whether material, mental, spiritual, or in the form of family, friends, colleagues, teammates, classmates, objects and things you hold dear, all support you in some way. We don't need just one layer of support; we need as many as we can get.

When we are not supported, we feel alone and go to the dark side of our internal states. This lack of support can destroy our belief in this crucial second layer of resilience, Supportive Structures. Love is a key component. However, we can learn to love our self and create support from within. This is a difficult task, especially for someone who has not been well supported early in life. Sometimes we just need to look for the support that's already there or ask for more. When support shows up, we have to embrace it and help put it into place so that we become a part of the process.

Supporting our self is the most crucial element. We can support our self once we become more aware of the support we actually have. A great way to understand this is to be of service, to help others on their journeys so that the help we seek also comes looking for us. We must find it in our hearts to recognize when someone is seeking help and figure out what it is they need. This requires a great deal of empathy and awareness.

Support needs a feedback loop. Imagine a metal pole stuck into the ground. Over time, wind and elements can soften the ground and the pole will eventually topple from wind or rain. However, if I pour concrete around it, tie ropes to the top and stake them into the ground and perhaps paint the pole with element-proof paint, that one pole will not waver in harsh conditions. We can continue to build on this idea and create more support for this one pole. You get the idea: the more support, the more we are reassured our pole will not topple.

A HOME IN HELL

WE ARRIVED AT THE REFUGEE CAMP AND WAITED IN LINE
for supplies. A tent, approximately ten feet by twenty feet,
was to become home until further notice. Guards and teams
with the United Nations gave us supplies and pointed on
a map, showing us where we could set up our tent along
a grid. The intent was to build neighborhoods where they

could separate families from single men, essentially creating two camps. We walked over half a mile to find a stake in the ground with the number twenty-two on it.

My teenage brothers and my dad went to work, trying to figure out how to put the tent together before nightfall. They used their bare hands to dig holes and gathered stones and mud to anchor the posts. Once the posts were finally up, they could lay the massive sheet of canvas over the tent to pitch it. The tent came with a second piece of fabric to be used as our carpet. This canvas sheet was the only thing between us and the dirt ground.

We finally took a moment to eat dinner together before the sunset. The food was military MRE (meals ready to eat) given to us when we got our tent. It was a packaged brown box, filled with random food I had never seen before. A sauce that tasted like apples, dried rice and meatballs covered in tomato sauce. A small square of cheese and a slice of bread that tasted awful. The best part of this package was the small candy bar. I longed for the warm, chewy "khbuz," or pita, my grandma made in bundles in her tandoor oven. I wanted some kebabs on rice and lentil soup, the delicious meals my mom whipped up.

The temperature began to drop, and night took over. After we all finished eating, the exhaustion hit. Using the few blankets and pillows we were given, we all squished together to stay warm. I could hear women and men crying in the distant background. The energy of the pain and suffering was everywhere, but we were lucky to be alive. Sleep was a gift; we all felt a sense of calm as we could no longer hear the bombs and gunshots. Though we were in a tent far from home, we were together.

Morning came around quickly. My body was achy and sore, and my brain was foggy. I believed for a moment that I had an insane dream. I saw my father up early and doing his morning prayer. His prayer regimen was a reassuring sign that I was safe with family. I looked up and saw the tent we had spent all day building and realized I wasn't dreaming. This was now my reality.

* * *

The desert kills: it kills anyone who doesn't think water is the most critical resource. Water is king, and nothing in the world is as essential for our survival. The cold temperatures at night dipped below freezing, and the days felt like we were in a sauna that wouldn't turn off.

My three older brothers had to walk four miles every morning to a large water tank at the center of the camp to get water for all nine of my family members. They waited in line for hours and were allowed only two five-gallon containers per person. After, they lugged the full containers the four miles back. This water was essential for our survival; we used it for cooking, bathing, and drinking.

Semitrucks brought in food and supplies roughly once every week. There was no guarantee that certain foods would show up. Just like the water, we had to stand in line for hours to collect what we could. If we were lucky, we would get meat on certain days, and vegetables, rice, and canned food on others. Our kitchen consisted only of camping supplies, small pots and pans, and utensils. My mother, the backbone of our family, was a miracle worker, doing her best to make sure we were fed and healthy. Cooking up rice and making chicken skewers, using canned foods to mix in a vegetable soup. Beans and tuna were always on the menu as most of our canned food was tuna. It was gross to eat this all the time, but she took that stuff, mixed it on a skillet with salt and tomatoes, and put it together with some pita, making sandwiches to fill our bellies. She did her best to make the food taste as good as it could.

After a month at the camp, our hope that Saddam's regime would fall had started to diminish. The depth of despair among the people at the camp was palpable. We didn't know how long we would have to stay, or how much longer we could live in such extreme conditions.

One day around this time, my brothers and I took a walk around the camp and found a man making mud bricks. The bricks were the size of cinder blocks. He poured mud into forms he made from wood planks, let them sit for a few hours, and then repeated the process.

"What are you doing?" my brother Alaa asked.

"The winter will be relentless," the man said. "If we don't build proper walls, we could die from the cold weather."

We realized we needed to build walls, too, and quickly.

Alaa asked if the man could teach us. He showed us how he collected excess water from cleaning dishes and showers and mixed it with the clay dirt underneath the soft sand at our feet. He dug out a three-foot-by-three-foot hole and would add water to the dirt and stomp on it to get the substance to compound itself. Once it began to be malleable, he poured the mixture into a rectangle form that was the size of a shoebox.

We studied every step until we mastered the process. For hours, as my older brothers poured water into the pit over the stand, my brother Mohammed and I stomped on the dirt to turn it into firm clay. I liked being a part of the process and feeling like I could help my big brothers. We stretched the tent we were given when we first arrived over the top of the structure and anchored the ropes to the dirt ground. In the final step, we stuffed the nooks and crannies with mud clay to make sure bugs and insects wouldn't get in.

Weeks of making these bricks and building one wall after another, our refugee tent had gotten a significant upgrade—a tiny clay home, built with pure sweat, blood, and tears. Four big walls created the main living room, and next to it was another open area for a tiny kitchen. My brothers also dug up the ground and connected the bathroom to a septic tank, so we could have a toilet. For nine people, the space was tight, but it was our home for the time being.

Our home in Iraq was familiar, cozy, and adorned with Islamic scripture, paintings, photos. Running water and a steady stream of electricity. The call to prayer over the city created a calming time for all to pray. The sweet taste of chai and cardamom filled cups into the evening with relatives hanging out sharing stories and poetry. This place was nothing like home; all I could hear and see was the sadness in people's voices and eyes.

One day, while my older brothers were waiting in line for water, a yelling match turned into a fight between a Saudi Arabian guard and a refugee. Anger was running high, and the waiting was becoming unbearable. The guard had harassed the refugee's wife, who was waiting in the women's line. A large crowd formed, and more men started fighting. Yas, the second oldest brother, tried to pull away, but more men around him began to shove, scream, and fight one another. The Saudi Arabian military guards rushed to the crowd and arrested everyone in the fight, including Yas.

We didn't know what happened to him, and when he

would return, if ever. My mother and father hardly slept for the next few days as we all waited for news. Yas was the family poet, always singing and reciting poems in his incredible voice. The silence in our home was painful. My father tried very hard to plead with some guards, but they wouldn't give him any information.

We found out later Yas was put in a jail cell with a few dozen men and beaten up for hours on end. The beatings continued for three days straight. The jail cell was punishment. The Saudi guards wanted to let these men know who was in charge.

Finally, they dropped Yas off about eight miles away from the camp, in the middle of the barren, scorching desert. It was the final blow of their punishment. Somehow, he didn't get lost and made it home by dark. When we saw his figure in the distance, we ran to greet him. He laid down on the ground and started heaving. The whole family could feel his suffering. We were all in tears. The camp was already a living hell, and this made it worse.

My father entertained us with stories and tons of comedic references to theater and movies to keep our minds off of our current predicament. He would act out silly gestures and used a variety of voices to make funny jokes about our lives. He changed his accent to an Egyptian one and mimicked a famous actor named Adel Imam, turned his eyes to look cross-eyed and said things like, "Where's the way back home? I've been walking in circles for days," crossing his arms and pointing in two directions. Any time he saw one of us down or not feeling well, he would recite a verse from the Quran to ensure us that the days ahead would be much better than the days that had passed. He encouraged us not to lose faith. His hope kept our family's hope alive. Allah had a bigger plan for us, he said. "We just need to be patient to seek refuge in another country."

I slept on a folded blanket and was covered by another blanket that ran across my brother Mohammed and me. I slept only a few feet away from where my mother and father slept. Being a light sleeper, I typically heard my father waking up to do his pre-prayer ablution outside of our tent. Though he tried to be quiet, I would hear him sometimes, and when I would get up, he would wink at me and smile, a sign for me to go back to sleep and that everything was OK.

Every morning he woke up at four thirty to pray, asking Allah, with absolute sincerity, for the strength to endure the day ahead.

THE SCHOOL OF RULES

MY FATHER BURST THROUGH THE OPENING IN THE tent and smiled big before announcing the United Nations was building a school for all the kids from kindergarten to high school. This was huge. My father had been trying to teach us the alphabet, reading and writing and some math on a weekly basis. But it was never consistent, and having no books to try to teach from, it was even more difficult. There was a school that the refugees put together combining a few tents, but it was very crowded and too far to walk to on a daily basis.

At six years old, I was so ready to start anything that even resembled a legitimate school with a daily schedule.

On my first day, I waited for hours as they passed out books and backpacks and a few supplies, surrounded by kids I had never met or seen before. The girls and the boys were assigned to separate classrooms. When I walked into my classroom, I saw the other students sitting on the ground. There were no tables or chairs. I smiled and walked to the back, sat on the ground, faced the blackboard, and waited for the teacher to speak.

The teacher started the session by telling us all to be silent and only speak when asked. He wrote all the rules on the blackboard. We had to get up in front of the class and write down words and full sentences, read out loud from our workbooks, and turn in our homework on time every day. If we didn't follow the rules, we would be punished. I swallowed a big gulp. It was serious.

After our class, we got a ten-minute break, and the next teacher arrived for our Quran reading session. This teacher was as strict as the guy before, if not more. I don't remember him ever smiling. For four hours, we sat and listened to the teachers give us our first lessons until it was time for a thirty-minute break to eat. I went outside and walked to the edge of the school. A big fence was separating us from the infinity of the desert. I sat down on the ground, ate the sandwich and apple my mother had packed, and stared at the school in pure fear.

The days and weeks went on, and school became more intense. Most of these teachers were brutal to kids. Some of the teachers were Saudis, and others were Iraqi teachers who were also refugees. They smacked me, they hit me, threw erasers at me, and they humiliated students in front of the whole class if we didn't know the answers to questions or didn't do our homework. I was young and school was hard, so hard. I disliked almost every teacher, and the classrooms always smelled like cigarettes. The smell of their nasty cologne, mixed with their body odor and cigarettes, made the teachers even more unbearable. They thought they were good teachers, but they acted more like generals of an army.

There was only one teacher I liked—my art teacher, who was a friend of my dad's. He taught with a kind spirit and encouraged me to be curious and adventurous. He taught me drawing and perspective and how to use a calligraphy pen. I loved using a calligraphy pen and seeing how pushing and releasing the pressure made for thicker and thinner lines. Rolling the pen gently between my thumb and index finger to create the body and connection between letters and words. Breathing softly and exhaling while I dragged the pen across the page to practice letters. I was in a meditative state when I practiced art and drawing there; time seemed to go so fast. I loved the precision and focus, the flow of ink and watching it dry in the seconds after I wrote my name.

In science class, however, my grades were terrible, and I struggled to understand the concepts. The teacher ruled with an iron fist. I was so busy feeling scared of doing something wrong, I would freeze up and not learn a thing.

* * *

A year of school went by and it felt like an eternity in some loophole of hell. My fears grew more, and my insecurities turned into being mute in the back of class, avoiding eye contact and trying hard not to be noticed. I would say a bundle of words throughout the whole day. I barely spoke to anyone. I was afraid to speak, afraid to say something wrong and get punished. I doodled cartoon characters that came and saved me from these days. I drew cartoon heroes beating up all the teachers and taking me out of the camp altogether.

The last thing we had to do as second-graders was take a test to get into third grade, covering all that we learned throughout the year. I wasn't sure I could pass the test; I got by, but I hardly listened.

When I took the test, I did OK on most of it—reading, writing, and surprisingly OK with math. I failed the science section in the most epic way. I felt dumb and ashamed, that something was wrong with me, that I couldn't keep this material in my mind. I was terrified of how I would explain to my parents that I failed. Most of all, I didn't want to show my sister, Zainab, my grade, as she had been working so hard to help me study.

I cried my face off while walking home. I didn't know what to do. I finally made it to our compound and broke the news about my grades. Seeing my puffy eyes and red cheeks, Zainab and my father asked me what happened. My eyes started to well up again. I told them I had failed. I could only move on to the third grade if I took a summer test. Otherwise, I'd have to repeat the second grade all over again.

"OK," my dad said simply. "You will learn, and you will pass."

My sister held me accountable to sit and study. Every morning during the whole summer, my face was buried in a science book. I learned everything, from how rainbows form to how trees make oxygen. I memorized every single question and every possible answer. I got so good that Zainab would ask me about a page or how clouds form and I would answer almost verbatim what the text said.

I understood the material because she showed me the science beyond the textbook. She would take me outside the tent and use our overhead tank that had water in it and attach it to a hose. Then using her thumb, she created pressure so the water would spray and create a drizzle effect. The sun would hit it and create a mini-rainbow effect, teaching me how sunlight plays an effect on water.

We tried to grow a few sunflowers and we watered them

daily to try to keep them alive, but it was just too hot. Still, I understood the concept of soil and how it provides nutrients to plants. She would then ask me to draw diagrams so that I could show her what I understood from our lessons. My mind absorbed what I was reading even more.

When the test day came, I was ready. I knew the textbook inside and out. My mom made a delicious breakfast. I was full, happy, and ready to smash the test. Before entering the portable classroom, I waved to my dad and my sister. The teacher handed out the examination. I read every question carefully and slowly. I knew the answers as fast as I could read them. I turned my exam in first and sat back down while the teacher graded it. Twenty minutes later, he called me back up.

"We will see you in third grade," he said, handing me back my test.

My eyes lit up, and I smiled from ear to ear. I ran out of the classroom and jumped up and down. My sister and dad hugged and congratulated me.

"See," my dad said, "if you work hard, you can celebrate after." We stopped by a small market and got some sweets and baklava to celebrate. My mom had prepped some chicken and rice for dinner. It was one of the happiest days of my life at the refugee camp so far.

My sister Zainab celebrated my small wins at the end of every week by ensuring that I got a candy bar. Laughing and joking with me released the anxiety. My support structures were intact; they had been and would continue to be around me. My feedback loop was developing with my siblings in unique ways. I recognized the support I had around me was the love of my family. The love and support were powerful and just as important as the fabric tents that kept the harsh elements outside.

SOMETHING OUT OF NOTHING

TWO YEARS AFTER LIVING IN THE MUD-BRICK UNIT my brothers put together, we moved to a bigger camp. Located a few miles away from our original camp, but still in the middle of the desert surrounded by a fence and barbed wire. A prison for refugees, this camp was made up of rows of rectangular units. Each had its own water tank and a small open courtyard. One of these new concrete boxes became our home. We even had electricity for a few hours a day. The improvements provided a bit more security from the harsh climate. Our refugee camp was starting to feel more like a small town.

My brothers were always hustling, either trading or borrowing to get things for my mom or the latest copy of a new movie. This is what everyone did in the camp, bartering for one thing or another, trying to survive the days. One day, they came home with a small television and an

Atari system. Later, they scored dubbed copies of movies like *Rambo* and *Terminator*. We loved watching Hollywood and Bollywood movies together in the family room.

The electricity came on in the evening for a couple of hours. After dinner and prayer, we gathered to watch movies or hang in the courtyard, telling stories. Poetic words flowed from my mom as she poured tea: *"When the desert night folds over our head like a blanket in the cold, the sparkles of stars remind us to where we return, the heavens await us, while we dream of tomorrow's meal. We are the survivors, the desert dwellers, seeking our destiny to unroll like carpets for prayer."*

Her depth with words went further than I could understand, but the rhythm in her voice had a beautiful melody. My father would share stories and joke with us as we sipped tea and listened around a small fire. Words of our Prophet Mohammed on the importance of seeking knowledge and the cave in which he would mediate for years until he met the Angel Gabriel. The importance of fasting, and speaking about his followers, the Imams, the scholars, our descendants; stories of battles and bravery would fill the air. We dozed off into the night praying and hoping for a brighter future.

With little resources to make toys, our creativity flowed. We made what we could with what we had. Trash bags, some sticks, and thread were excellent materials for kites. My brother Ghazwan, also known as Ozzie, the fourth oldest, built kites with precision and quality along with a paper chain tail. He handed me the string and gave it a few feet and told me to take off running to catch the wind. We flew kites for hours, trying to squeeze in as much fun as we could before the sun went down.

Ozzie and I played through the making of games, kites, soccer balls, and whatever else we could find and turn into a toy or a game. He would tie a garbage bag around my neck, loosely of course, to make me believe I was a superhero. He had so much love for animals and would tell me stories of his baby goat that he missed in Iraq. He had a gap-tooth smile that would fill rooms with energy.

I looked up to my older brother Mohammed, too; he was fifth in the line of children. He is three years older, and I was basically his shadow while we wandered the streets around our camp. He was a tough kid and was always looking out for me. A lot of kids running around the neighborhood were always getting into trouble. Mohammed didn't want me to run around with these kids alone, knowing that they would sway me to do stupid stuff.

I did whatever I could to tag along with my older brothers. I loved entertaining them with heroic stories that I would dream up on our walks. I would tie an empty trash bag around my neck and make a cape and pretend that I was going to fly us out of the camp once I gained my powers. I wanted to save us from the camp and was always asking them what they thought my superpowers were going to be. They asked how I was going to defeat the guards at the gate. "I would run really fast and punch them all at once and tie all of them together and sling shot them far in the desert!" I said. They laughed and entertained my imaginative schemes.

My youngest sister Heba (last of all the Al-Baiaty children), Mohammed, and I always hung out together, trying to come up with something to do. We collected bags and stuffed them into one another to try to make a soccer ball. We piled up some rocks about eight feet apart to make a goal, drew a goalie box in the dirt, and played soccer. In a matter of minutes, more kids from the neighborhood joined to play. We kicked up dust, making a ruckus. We busted our toes on rocks, wearing nothing but flip-flops. That was our fun for the day.

During times of Eid or holidays, the camp would be full of these boxy military-green Volkswagen Vanagons and trucks driving around tossing toys and candy bars out of the back. Mohammed, Heba, and I would chase these vans down to ensure we scored something on Eid days. The level of dehumanization here was at the very lowest. It would have been just as easy to line kids up and hand something to them to make them feel good for once. No, they made us chase and fight for what was rightfully ours while they laughed and taunted us.

* * *

My mom's brother Ali came over often to hang out with us. Uncle Ali was in the military, and when the war started, he wanted nothing to do with fighting for Saddam. A few of his friends tossed away their military gear and got into civilian outfits when the war broke out. He had made his way to the refugee camp around the same time we did. At the camp, he ran a little mini-mart at the end of our complex that he built out of corrugated metal and mud bricks. It was the convenience store for the neighborhood and also where he slept. He would come over to our concrete box often to eat breakfast, lunch, and dinner.

Uncle Ali was always up to something. He either owed people money, or they owed him money. He always had some hustle that involved selling cigarettes or heavy painkillers. He could get you pretty much anything if you gave him a few days. From the markets a few miles away, he bought wholesale cigarettes, candy, soda, and other little things people at the camp needed. At random times, he showed up with treats or gifts. He always asked me if I wanted or needed anything, and I would ask for a Safari candy bar from his mini-mart. But one day, I asked for something bigger. I wanted a bike. I had been seeing kids with bicycles around the neighborhood.

"I will turn this camp upside down and shake it to get you a bike," Uncle Ali promised.

A few weeks later, I came home from school and Uncle Ali shouted, "You're here!" He grabbed a bicycle leaning on the wall.

My new bike was three bikes made into one. Sure, it had some scuffs here and there, but I loved it for its character. The bike was an army green color, with a banana seat and low handles.

It was the perfect size for me, but I had a big problem. I didn't know how to ride a bicycle.

My brother Yas offered to teach me. He got me outside and got me to hop on the bike. He instructed me to look out into the distance, and not look at my feet. I struggled to keep the bike upright. "Start pedaling and to try to keep the handlebars straight," he ordered.

He grabbed the back of the banana seat and gave me a slight push as I pedaled for the first time. I was catching a good rhythm, and my bike started moving faster. I couldn't stop laughing from my excitement. We went up and down the complex while he held onto the seat. As he ran beside me, I yelled, "Don't let go yet! Don't let go yet!"

But he had already let go about thirty yards back. I was on my own, riding a bike within an hour of learning. I kept falling and scuffing up my knees and the palms of my hands, but I didn't care.

LAYER 3

DISCIPLINED PATIENCE

MY FATHER AND I WALKED AROUND A LOT DURING our time in the camp. He constantly repeated lines from the Quran, our Prophet Mohammed, (pbum) or the Prophet's descendants, the Imams. Some stuck, some had no meaning to me. One, however, seeped very deep into my subconscious. He used it a lot when I would get irritable, frustrated, or jealous of my friends or siblings when they got something I wanted and couldn't get. He would hold both of my hands and look me in the eye.

"Hussein, remember what I taught you the other day?"

"Yes, Baba."

"Do you remember the words?"

"Yes, Baba."

"What are they?"

"Imam Ali taught us that two things define you: your patience when you have nothing, and your gratitude when you have everything."

"OK, Habibi, you will have it. Have patience and it will come."

I can hear him saying this to me right now even as I write. It's one of my favorite sayings of all time. These words pierce through time and space and are a constant reminder for me to dig deeper into this third layer of resilience.

Once we've put the supportive structures in place, we can now lay down the foundation for patience. Patience is not found in anyone or a specific place. Only you can define what it means to you through your own experiences. I discovered patience through the discipline my father exemplified throughout my childhood in the refugee camp.

This unique layer is one that may take you years to uncover further, but like all other layers, it's within us to access, and the more we do, the more we have. Once you come to realize that pretty much everything is out of your control, you will come to be more patient. The only thing you can control is your time and how you choose to spend it to cultivate patience.

Patience is not about waiting around for some result to happen. It's rather the opposite: working with intent and calculated purpose. Using the spice of discipline and a grateful attitude, you can develop a daily practice that will ensure you get closer to your outcome in the right space and at the right time. The rest is left to the universe. For now, enjoy the sweetness that comes from practicing patience with discipline.

ESCAPE THROUGH ART

TIME PASSING AT THE REFUGEE CAMP WAS LIKE watching sand trickle through an hourglass. Having a job or a reason to get up and do something was so important.

My father and I took long walks through the refugee camp. He would pick up torn pieces of tents, roll them, bring them back home, and stack them up against a wall. The thick, military-grade canvas was too good to pass up. He wanted to archive the madness of living in a refugee camp. The canvas could tell our story.

When we fled, he had taken a small bag full of oil paint colors and brushes. He knew he would have the itch to paint, and not having his supplies would drive him crazy. He cleaned each piece of canvas well and hung them to dry. While they were drying, he sketched out what he was going to paint. After, he examined his sketch and pushed the pencil around to see if he needed more eye-catching details. He laid out his paint supplies and carefully considered which colors to use.

When he was ready, he laid the canvas on the ground and drew with a light pencil. Once the raw canvas was ready for painting, he stopped for a break. Eating dinner and doing his evening prayer were crucial before he started.

When we all started to go to bed in the late evening, he began to paint late into the night by candlelight. I tried to stay awake to watch, but most of the time, I would fall asleep. While we slept, he pushed something necessary out of himself—a way to cope with what was happening in his life. When we woke up the next morning, I looked over to see what he had painted. Big blotches of circular patterns, all very dull colors.

I asked, "Baba, why does your painting look messy and what are you painting?"

"Be patient; it will show itself to you soon," he replied.

Needing to focus and quiet my chatter, he sketched a picture of Mickey Mouse and asked me to replicate it. The three circles first, the eyes, the mouth, and the smile. I did a replica drawing and it wasn't bad. He told me to redraw the cartoon as many times as possible to fill up a whole page. When I filled up the whole page, he told me to draw Mickey in different positions, or doing things like running, holding a book reading, or dancing around. I could draw Micky Mouse blindfolded I drew him so much. He pushed me to shade and use color and taught me how to channel my imagination through my hand.

* * *

One afternoon in the summer of 1993, the whole refugee compound got word about a weapons search. This was typical and could last for days. The army conducted random monthly searches to ensure that people didn't make homemade weapons.

At this point, three years into our stay, my father felt like he had nothing to lose and decided to display his art. He usually hid his art out of my mother's fears that they would arrest him for making political pieces. My mother begged him not to, and my brothers did too, convinced he would end up in jail. My mother cried, and my brothers cringed when the soldiers knocked on our doors. Something deep inside made my father not want to listen. He couldn't imagine he'd be taken away for some paintings he had done out of scraps of tents. He believed displaying his art could lead to a sale or, better yet, a connection to help us get out of the camp.

The soldiers knocked on the door for a second time. He looked up and whispered a prayer to Allah to help guide him and ease the situation into a positive one. The third knock was even louder. He took another step to open the door to greet the soldiers.

"Assalamu Alaikum," he said with a big smile and a welcoming gesture.

"Are you the man of the household?" they asked.

"Yes," my father replied. Four men came into our small home, and another eight or so waited outside around the trucks. My father asked how they were doing, making small talk, as the men prepared to search. Had they had a chance to take a break? Did they want to have lunch with us?

The men looked at him funny and replied, no, thank you, but some water would be great. He was warming them up. They began looking through our three-room unit.

"Would you like to report any issues from around the camp? Is anyone causing harm or danger to others?" they asked.

"Not that I know of. We keep to ourselves and stay out of trouble," my father replied. He asked if they wanted to stay a few extra minutes for some tea and some homemade baklava. They gathered in a huddle before one of them said, "Sure, tea sounds good."

After a few minutes, small talk turned into a conversation. My mother prepared Iraqi cardamom chai, dark black with raw sugar with a hint of cinnamon. The chai came right on time as my dad primed them to tell more stories. The soldiers shared a bit about who they were, what tribes they belonged to, and how often they visited Mecca. My father began to make jokes and tell his own story. He was an artist and had several gallery shows in Baghdad. He had once even been commissioned to make a mural for Saddam Hussein himself.

The men's interest was piqued. They kept asking for more of Saddam Hussein's stories, and to see my father's art. My father had plenty of stories to entertain the soldiers. The soldiers responded with laughter and began to relax. One of the men went outside and asked the other men to weapon search in the next two units, so they could stick around.

After taking a deep breath, my father asked if they had a few more minutes to see his work.

They were confused, wondering how he had managed to bring his paintings with him from Iraq. My father clarified that he had painted them at the camp, with scraps of materials and a few things he had brought with him when he fled.

My father asked my brother Mohammed and me to bring out a few paintings. His portrait of the King of Saudi Arabia was spot-on. The soldiers couldn't believe what they were seeing. They asked to see more, and Mohammed and I kept bringing out his canvas paintings. My father had turned our space into a gallery. He offered more tea and conversation.

They asked him if he did commission work and his rates. My father said he would be happy to take on commission work, he just needed some supplies and an up-front payment.

One soldier bought the painting of the king, and another soldier asked my father if he could paint a second one. This was my father's first commission work he had in years. He was ready to start putting his painting skills to real use.

A few days later, the same men showed up at our door with the art supplies my father had asked for. Three large fresh white canvases, oil paint supplies, and pictures of what they wanted to be painted. One asked for a painting of himself against a desert backdrop. The other wanted a portrait of his kids.

With a new set of paintbrushes and boxes full of oil paint, my dad was ready to work. He laid out three canvases and worked on them simultaneously. He painted the foundation colors on one piece. While that was drying, he painted the foundation on another. For hours on end, he primed each canvas.

After dinner, I watched as he painted with relentless focus. Time does not affect a man who is on a mission. He was determined to get us out of the camp. At the same time, he kept working on his own paintings of desert scenes, floral patterns intermixed with Arabic poetry and Arabic calligraphy. Within the month, he had finished the soldiers' paintings, and they were ready for pickup.

The men showed up with more friends to meet my father. They sat out in our courtyard and started to converse while Mohammed brought out my mother's Iraqi chai they so loved, along with some baklava. After catching up for a while, my dad got up to go to his room to get the paintings. He brought them out one after the other and leaned them against the wall.

The group became silent for a few moments. They all smiled and said, "Mashallah, remarkable." One of them kept looking at the photo and back at the painting, again and again, and asked, "How did you make the painting better than the photo?"

"I imagined my kids in your picture and loved each one as if they were my own," my father said. "I poured love into it. The vibrancy of their smiles came to life even more."

The man began to cry. He hugged my father and crumbled the photo. He didn't need it anymore.

The next few months, he kept painting commissioned work while he painted work that archived our time in the camp. My father painted us flying kites, drinking tea, and laying down under the Milky Way. Commissioned work was great, but he preferred to paint from his soul, which at this time was experiencing extreme pain. These side paintings sometimes were purchased, too, but for him they were therapy sessions. These paintings told daily life and political stories and showed the truth about our lives in the refugee camp.

Every few weeks, more soldiers would show up with friends. Whether it was higher-ups or generals, they were eager to greet my dad. They began to bring over more oversized canvases and more supplies.

One day, a man came with an entourage of Hummers and over fifteen soldiers. He was important, but no one knew how important. He came to meet my dad; he heard so many great things about this artist. He introduced himself as Khalil Iben Al Gemel. He ran the refugee camp.

My father asked him to have a seat in our courtyard. Some of his soldiers stayed outside, and some came in with him. Khalil was very interested in my dad's story and how we fled Iraq. His eyes filled up with tears as my father described the few years of living in the camp. He asked about the paintings and how they came to be.

"I have no choice, my family needs to live," my father explained. "If paintings can bring in a little money, that's what I will do." My brother Mohammed and I set an array of paintings up against the wall. The canvas paintings were all different sizes, full of color, texture, emotion, and story. Khalil was a collector of art and noticed the amount of courage my father put into his work.

"It has not been easy waiting for the immigration process to move along. Painting allows me to deal with this loss of time. It is my therapy and helps me meet new people." Khalil nodded in understanding. My father continued, "You may think I'm painting from a place of pleasure, but these paintings come from pain, from a deep concern that my family may never leave this place."

My dad asked if he had kids. Khalil told him he had eleven beautiful kids.

"Would you let them live in this camp with us?" my father

asked boldly. Khalil replied, "This is no place for anyone. I will do my best to help you and your family."

Khalil pulled my dad to the side and gave him some money. He wanted to buy a few pieces and commission a portrait. He handed my dad a photograph of his entire family: eleven kids, ranging from babies to grown adults, himself, and his wife. Khalil asked one of his soldiers to bring in supplies. The soldiers brought a canvas eight feet wide and six feet tall along with two boxes of brushes and oil paint. It was my father's most massive canvas yet.

My father studied the photograph closely and said, "You have a beautiful family. It would be my honor to paint them for you."

My dad had been waiting for an opportunity like this since we got here. That evening, we had a great dinner with a dish my mother called maklouba, "the upside down." It was filled with rice, eggplant, peas, and canned veggies all mixed with beef and sprinkles of curries and spices. She prepared a lentil soup to go with it that made me want to eat my fingers just to get more of the taste. She cooked up handmade pita bread; though we didn't have a tandoor to give it the perfect fluff, she made it so soft with her cooking magic. Dinner hit so hard, I didn't remember eating this good and laughing so hard from all the storytelling. Everyone's spirits were high. My father started us off with a prayer from the Quran, and we shut our eyes to listen. He thanked Allah for keeping us all alive, healthy, and away from harm. We went to bed with a new sense of hope and admiration for our father. The candlelight of optimism was beginning to flicker once again.

For the next two months, I watched my father make something remarkable. He woke up before everyone else, did his morning prayer, and sat in front of the large canvas all day. He took a break only for lunch and the afternoon call to prayer, before getting back to his canvas painting until dinner. Often, tears would come to him as he prayed Quranic scriptures through whispers. The transfer of energy, from his body to the painting, was constant. Over the days and weeks, I watched as the figures came to life.

The painting was extensive and took two months to complete. Each figure needed hours of foundation and layers of details. He would often tilt his head back and forth, eyeing the painting from all sides to ensure the canvas had balance. When he took a few steps back, he asked me to stand where he was. He told me to look at the edges of the painting and focus on where the eye wants to go. He made me point to this area and explain why. I loved being a part of the process because I felt like I was helping in some way.

While my father painted, the official documentation we had been waiting for arrived. We needed to be approved by a line of higher-ups in the immigration processes in order to be eligible to have an interview to leave the camp. Certain people, such as those with ill family members, got verified documentation a bit faster. Having a big family with girls also helped you get out because of potential sexual assault or abuse. In our case, my father's art and having a big family helped our case move forward.

Families around us had been leaving for the past few years to other countries, which made the waiting process so difficult to bear. At times, it just seemed like the luck of the draw. We finally saw our name on the central board. Our interview with the United Nations for refugee resettlement was in sight.

All I could think about was what it would be like to live in America. The fast cars, the movie stars I would get to meet, like Arnold and the guy from *Rambo*. I could take karate classes. The movies we watched informed my daydreams. I thought everyone must live in big houses and drive Lamborghinis and Ferraris.

When the painting was finished, Khalil showed up with soldiers and friends to pick it up. They all came into our courtyard area and sat on the rug to have tea and catch up. My dad brought everyone into the back room where he had been painting. When Khalil saw the finished piece, his jaw dropped. A few moments of silence passed before anyone said anything.

"The painting is perfect," Khalil said, shaking his head in disbelief. He gazed into the painting, taking steps forward and backward to try to grasp the whole piece. He walked over to my father and hugged him.

The soldiers wrapped and packed up the painting and loaded it into a military truck for Khalil. Before Khalil left, he and my dad had a conversation about the potential good news. Our case was moving along, and we should have our United Nations refugee resettlement interview soon. Khalil made good on his deal and paid my dad the rest of the money for the painting.

That was the last time I saw Khalil and his entourage. The money my dad earned for the painting was all that we had for our journey ahead.

SWEETNESS OF PATIENCE

———

AFTER A MONTH MORE OF WAITING, WE FINALLY GOT to sit for our refugee resettlement interview. A translator and an American man and woman sat across from us.

They asked a variety of questions about our health and family. I sat and stared at the woman's blond hair and blue eyes. The man had brown hair and fair skin. I hadn't seen blond hair or blue eyes in my life. The woman had a shawl on, but it wasn't a hijab like my mother wore. It hung loosely off of her head, and I saw blond hair for the first time in my life and wondered if she painted it.

They told us a church was sponsoring refugee families to come to the United States. We could take as long as we needed to reimburse them. It was a deal no one could refuse.

They offered to send us to Miami, Florida. There was a vast art scene there, they said, knowing my father was an artist. But my dad asked if we could go where we knew someone who could help us get on our feet. My dad's uncle, Hadi, had been a refugee at the camp and left two years ago to go to a place called Portland, Oregon.

That was our final conversation with the United Nations Resettlement Team that would decide our fate.

Being patient at the refugee camp had never been easy. Now that there was an end in sight, it was even harder. The joy of leaving the camp clashed with the bitter taste of leaving so many friends and family behind. My uncle Ali and all our other relatives at the camp would not be coming with us. They would have to wait their turn to seek refuge in another country. My dad fought hard for them during our interview process, but there wasn't much anyone could do except try to put in a good word for one another.

We got word we would take the caravan buses out of the camp in a week. Leaving was no longer a daydream.

We had a few more dinners with relatives and friends. Everyone was excited for us to go but also sad we would be apart on our journey out of the camp. My family stayed up late, carrying on conversations, packing the goods we would take with us, and giving away the rest of our goods.

The morning of our departure, I woke up early to the sound of my mother zipping up bags and shuffling things around. She asked me to wash up and get some breakfast with my younger siblings Heba and Mohammed. I jumped out of bed with excitement. We gathered our belongings on a bicycle pushcart and began walking the few miles to the gates of our camp, accompanied by some close family and friends.

We all hugged and cried on each other's shoulders. I began

to cry, too. I thanked my uncle for all the toys, games, and Safari candies. I was going to miss him and believed he would come after us in a few months. We all got on the buses and waved our Salaams to everyone. Watching hundreds of families pulled apart made the scene very difficult. We were the lucky ones who got to get out of the camp.

The buses began moving, and for the next six hours, we drove on a highway surrounded by desert as far as the eyes could see. There was nothing but yellow sand and blue sky.

The bus ride was long, but not as long as we'd been waiting for it. I got to sit with my older brothers, and they were cracking jokes, telling stories, and letting out sighs of relief. We all had no idea what awaited us but had fun daydreaming about a better life.

We finally made it to a transition facility. The place we stayed in was an upgraded version of our unit in the camp. Everything was clean and organized, with electricity, lights, and a TV. They held all of us at the small camp for a few days. I was confused. I thought we should be on a plane to the United States. My parents kept telling me that we would only be there for a couple of days.

After three days of medical examinations and more paperwork, I couldn't wait any longer. The excitement of getting on a plane was killing me. I couldn't wait to fly in the air; I couldn't wait to see America. My family all got on another bus, and after a few hours of driving, we arrived at a tiny airport. The authorities asked everyone to remain on the bus until they searched through all our bags. We sat there for yet another excruciating couple of hours.

Finally, a soldier got on the bus and yelled out, "Kamel Al-Baiaty!" My dad got up and walked to the front of the bus and then to the shelter where they were checking bags. Everyone panicked. We all thought something was wrong. After the longest half hour of our lives, my dad returned, smiling because everything was fine.

They had found six cases, filled with oil paint and his favorite brushes, and thought they were knives.

Once we were cleared, we went through security and took another shuttle for a short drive. When I first saw the aircraft, my eyes lit up. It was like a giant white spaceship that had come to rescue my family and me from the desert world.

I got to sit in a row close to my older sister Zainab and oldest brother Alaa. The airplane started the engines and positioned itself for takeoff. The aircraft began to speed up on the tarmac. We were in the air right as the sun was setting, on our way to a new home.

Our plane touched down on American soil on June 22,

1994. After an hour of waiting to get off, we went to a hold-ing area at JFK Airport in New York where the authorities could process our arrival. Through the windows, I people-watched and stared outside the window to see lines of airplanes. Endless questions roamed my mind. My mind was overloaded, and I stuck close to my older brothers for fear of getting lost in the crowds of people at the airport.

We got on one last plane to Portland, Oregon, where my dad's uncle Hadi, the one who made it to America before us and helped sponsor us, was awaiting our arrival. When we finally landed, it was around midnight. Great Uncle Hadi and his family greeted us with hugs, cries, and smiles. After endless hours of flying, waiting, transfers, and docu-mentation, we finally made it. I could see the worry come off my father's face, and my brothers start to relax.

We found our bags at baggage claim. I can still remember the layer of dust on the beaten bags from years of dragging them from one place to another. As we passed downtown Portland, I looked out the car window with a massive smile on my face. The buildings were all lit up at night. The whole city looked alive.

I felt like I was in the movie *Back to the Future 2*, where Marty, the main character, is in the future—seeing all the lights from the city, driving over the bridge and feeling like I was transported to another planet. A strange land, only familiar from movies I had seen. It was all new and so exciting. I couldn't wait to wake up the next morning and experience this new world around me. I couldn't believe we were here, in America, no longer bound by the endless desert and lack of resources.

LAYER 4

CREATIVE CONFIDENCE

WHILE I DON'T REMEMBER WHEN I FIRST STARTED walking, here is what I imagine went down: in the living room in our house in As-Samawah, I pull myself up by holding on to the edge of the couch looking back at my audience—my brothers, sisters, and my mom and dad. I smile, lose focus, and plop back on the floor. I try again, pulling myself up and looking back to make sure everyone was watching. This time, I take a step along the edge of the couch. I hear the claps; I hear the laughter. I take yet another step and a quick one after that. I'm excited, so much so, I lose focus and fall back down. I build up a rush in my body, so I get up and pull myself back up again. I look back, and my mom's arms are reached out, a few steps away. I can hear her say, "Yallah Habibi," guiding me into her arms. I let go of the couch and launch myself towards her, taking three, maybe four steps while I wobble on my chunky legs.

This was the moment I graduated from crawling to walking. For the past few weeks, I had been attempting the task without any luck. I fell on my butt, on my face, on my side, and even backward a few times where I let out some loud cries. The series of practice was daily, and I kept training to build my chunky thighs into weight-carrying machines.

When we are babies learning to walk, it isn't a question of if we can, but a matter of when.

Uncovering the next layer of resilience is a matter of believing in yourself and following through on your goals. Confidence is the tension between your practice and the moment of delivery. This layer needs a daily workout to keep it strong and vibrant and relies heavily on the ones prior to it. Creative confidence relies on your patience, your discipline, the strength of your supportive structures, and most of all, hope.

What do I mean by "creative confidence"? Being a human being requires creativity. Creativity is embedded in every single human. The issue is not whether or not you are creative, but whether you were taught how to uncover it. Perhaps someone told you that you're only creative if you think with your right brain. I get it. You were taught to fit into a box. You think since you're not in the arts, that you're not creative. But your mind is designed to problem solve, which is the essence of what it means to be creative. We all need the muscles of confidence to tap into our creativity.

GOING TO THE BEACH

———

IN EARLY SEPTEMBER 1994, I STARTED MY FIRST DAY of school. I had my backpack, some new jeans, and a t-shirt laid out and ready. Heba, my younger sister, was starting kindergarten, and I was starting third grade all over again.

As I walked through the hallways, a part of me couldn't believe where I was—in a school in America. I was amazed I had been assigned a female teacher, and I would be in class with girls. I had no idea what it would be like to sit next to a girl in school. When I walked into my classroom, the whole room stopped and paused and looked at me.

"Hello, I'm Mrs. Laurie. I'm your third-grade teacher. We are so excited you can join our classroom," my new teacher must have said. At the time, I heard a bunch of words in a language that I couldn't understand.

I looked up at her and smiled. "Thank you," I said. She responded with, "You're welcome," a word I actually understood, which made me feel good. She showed me where to hang my jacket and my new desk. The rest of the class became a blur, as I had no idea what anyone was saying. I sat quietly and observed as best as I could.

Recess came around, and I went outside and walked around the playground. I watched the other kids play. I had no idea what to do or say to join. I got on a swing and pushed myself around. I smiled to myself. I had been at school for already a few hours, and I hadn't seen anyone get hit by a teacher. I was so grateful to be sitting there, and not in a scorching desert full of fear.

In the cafeteria, I knew I had to be mindful of eating Halal meat. My father warned me to eat vegetarian at school. I didn't know how the system worked, so I followed other kids and stood in line to grab my tray and put food on it. Cheese pizza, salad, milk, juice, crackers, chips, fruit bowls—the options were endless. I put a pizza, juice, and some chips on my tray. When I got to the lunch lady, she asked me for a ticket. I looked back at her with a blank stare.

She pointed to the red tickets she was collecting.

I shook my head no.

"You need a red ticket to get food," she said. I left the tray and walked away, very bummed. I thought the food was free. I sat down on the edge of a table where some of my classmates were sitting. I thought we had to sit together. They looked at me funny, like "Why are you sitting here?" I didn't know what to do with myself other than sitting there and waiting for the bell to go off to go back to class.

When we finally went back to the class, one of the kids told the teacher that I didn't get any lunch. Mrs. Laurie gave me a banana and apple juice and asked if I was on free and reduced lunch. I shook my head from side to side, replying with an "I'm not sure" gesture.

She gave me a piece of paper and asked me to give it to my parents. It was an application for free and reduced lunch so that I could get those little red tickets. My sister Zainab and my cousin filled out the application the next day. I thought all the kids got free lunch, but it turned out it was for those kids whose families couldn't afford it.

The weeks began to fly by, and school was becoming overwhelming. I was trying to make sense of everything that was happening around me. I had never seen or played any of the games the other kids knew. I watched to see if I could pick them up.

I was too shy to talk to or be around girls. I tended to freeze up and smile. On a lucky day, a few girls came up and asked if I wanted to play kickball. I was suspicious. Girls don't ask boys to play. I joined the game and stood in line to wait my turn to kick the ball. I watched the other kids go up and listened to their conversation. I heard them say words like Disneyland, camping, skiing, and the beach. I stood there, unable to speak. My family had talked about driving out to the beach over a long weekend. I had never seen a beach before.

That night, I made my sister help me practice saying, "I'm going to the beach," over and over. With shaky hands and sweaty palms, I got up in front of my third-grade class.

"I'm going to the bitch!" I said really fast, with a big smile on my face. The whole class burst out laughing, and I knew I had said something wrong.

"You mean you are going to the 'beach,' right, Hussein?"

"Yes! Yes! Beach. Sorry, sorry," I shook my head and yelled.

All the kids laughed, and I felt like I should never open my mouth again or get up in front of another class. I started to enjoy school less. I was scared that I was going to do something wrong again and embarrass myself.

Managing my emotions while learning English was starting to get tricky. I was paying attention in class, turning my homework in, and smiling while doing it. I was trying to be hyper-aware and not make a sound and blend in. It all became too much, and at times I couldn't wait to get home and be in the safe environment of my family.

Not long after we moved to America, our home began to feel empty. At the camp, we were together a lot more as a family. I was always around my siblings. Now my mother and father were usually the only ones home. My older brothers had started classes and were working with IRCO, the Immigrant Refugee Community Organization that helps refugees get work and learn the culture. They were under a lot of pressure to get jobs and assimilate; they carried the burden of working and providing for our large family.

We had some relatives, people at IRCO, and Catholic Charities that helped. My brothers did their best and got many jobs, including day jobs at the Made in Oregon warehouse packing products. They began to get better at navigating around using public transportation. They worked the evenings as janitors for a Lebanese guy who owned a cleaning company. He picked them up in the late evening, and they would work all night, and we wouldn't see them until eight or nine in the morning the next day. They worked to clean up office buildings and businesses all over the Portland area. They had no time at all, with full-time jobs, learning English, and riding the Metro bus all over town.

THE DARN KID

BY THE TIME I GOT TO THE FIFTH GRADE, MY FAMILY
had moved three times, and I had changed schools every
time. My English had improved, and I could carry small
conversations and understand more. But when it came to
math, science, and writing, I struggled.

I tried my absolute hardest to memorize my multiplication
table. Trying to memorize the division was even worse.
Taking quizzes was like a nightmare to me. I wouldn't be
able to sleep the night before, obsessing over how bad I
was going to do. Because I was so nervous, I often avoided
studying and would do horrible as I predicted. My sister
Zainab was my constant savior, as she would often help
me study and do my homework.

At the refugee camp, I didn't like going to school or how
much the teachers beat us. But in America, I was allowed

to make mistakes. I could turn in homework and still have it half wrong. My teacher would try to help me understand the work, not beat me for being dumb. The fear became less overwhelming, and I started to be able to focus.

* * *

One afternoon, we went to go to the library for a special presentation by a children's book author. I sat and watched with interest. He demonstrated how he put human-like characteristics into cartoon animals. He did a lot of research on each animal to discover what makes them unique. By the end of this, he gave everyone an application and a letter to enter a book writing contest. I assumed the contest was an assignment for school. I thought to myself, how awesome is that!

I had a little over a month to complete and submit a book. I was motivated by the talk and how I could use my artistic abilities. My drawings were random collections of characters. I had notebooks full of drawings. I loved graphics but had no idea how to develop a character and tell a story. I immediately went home and told my father all about the speaker and the contest. All I had to do was come up with a story and draw it out. I needed some markers and specialty paper so I could start putting it together.

I came up with a story about a baby boy who loved basketball. He and his dad go to a basketball game. He wants an adult size basketball to bring home with him. At the game, the boy gets distracted and follows a rat into the bleachers. The boy ends up on the basketball court chasing the rat. He continues to chase the rat into the locker rooms, which leads him to a huge bin full of basketballs. He finds the perfect-sized basketball while his dad is searching for him. His dad finally finds him, and that's how the story ends. I named it "That Darn Kid," a play on the title of the movie, "That Darn Cat," which I had seen previews of on TV. I was ready to start drawing.

I started sketching the main character, a kid in a diaper. He gets into a lot of trouble but is fun and cute. He has big-framed glasses and crawls around bouncing a basketball, making a ruckus. Drawing one page at a time on sketch and trace paper took over two weeks. The hardest part was just getting started. I needed better paper and coloring markers to bring the kid to life and bring the whole book together.

I asked my dad to take me to the art store, where he spent fifty dollars on supplies for this book project. I know fifty dollars doesn't seem like a lot, but it is when you are on welfare and making ends meet. I knew I had to do a good job. I got premium drawing paper and some excellent soft markers that would blend when they mixed on top of one another. Like my dad taught me, I began tracing the original designs and got all the pages done. Every page was an art piece with detailed movement and color, which brought the story to life.

For hours on end, I colored in all the pages after school and doing my homework. When it came time to write the story, I needed to type it, cut out the small pieces of text, and glue them on the page. I made the cover using cardboard, wrapping it with red construction paper. I figured it would be easy to see it if it had a bright color. Also, red is my favorite color. It was the finishing touch. I was so excited to have it done, and I couldn't wait to submit it and see what books my friends had made, too.

On the day the book was due, I walked into class excited and ready to show my teacher the book. Mr. Atkins was sitting behind his desk and typing away on his computer before class started.

"I have finished the book for the school contest," I said, handing him the envelope with my prized book inside.

"What book contest?" he asked.

I reached into my backpack and pulled out the big yellow envelope with the application form. He smiled wide.

"You made a children's book!" He asked if he could look

through it. His eyes lit up at all the artwork. Every few pages, he would look up and say, "This is cool, Hussein. You did a great job!"

He told me he would submit it through the school and take care of the contest's shipping costs.

"It's not for school?" I asked.

"This is a national contest, and you are most likely the only kid from our school who is submitting a book!" I looked at him with a blank stare and then smiled.

"Only me?" I was still a bit confused. I was happy that I finished on time, and proud of it.

Mr. Atkins showed many of the kids in class my book. Some of them came up to congratulate me. For the first time in my life, I finally felt accomplished at school.

LAYER 5

ENVIRONMENTAL ADAPTATION

SWEAT POURING DOWN MY FOREHEAD, LIPS DRIED UP, THE sun beating down my neck. I sat down and got closer to my brother's feet to use his shadow. Yas looked down at me. "We're going to get water soon, Habibi." I sat in his shadow, anxiously waiting for the most precious resource known to man. I stood in line with my brothers, waiting for the Saudi Army Guard to release the water tank's valve. While we waited, droves of people pushed and shoved their way to the front of the line to get the liquid gold. "Yallah Akhi"—*Hurry, Brother!*—the man yells. My brother put down two five-gallon tanks, filled them up quickly, and sealed them tight. We got our share for the day and started our long four-mile walk back to the main camp.

My brothers set up a routine to take turns and meet each other halfway to ease the burden on one another. They adapted as best they could. We used water very carefully and didn't waste a drop of it. We made a few stops to rest, but we couldn't even drink the water yet. It needed to be boiled to kill off any bacteria. We finally made it back to our tent, and everyone was waiting. My mother boiled the water and let it sit for a while. Finally, we could drink warm water. I filled my cup and gulped it down. I felt it go down my throat and turn to instant energy to live to fight another day.

Water is holy in my life. I respect it immensely. This process of going to get water with my brothers made me appreciate this vital resource more than I could have ever imagined. Survival is all about doing a lot with a little. This experience made me develop a unique layer of resilience that resembles a fluid more than any other material. Adapting to the environment is much like an oasis in the desert. The fresh air, water, and break you need in your journey is found in the layer of adaptation. This layer gives life to all of the layers beneath and around it. Ensuring patience, the discipline has the sweetness of water after a long journey. Adjusting to a different environment is challenging. However, the benefits of change further enhance your lived experience and the missions to seek the next oasis of knowledge.

If I don't adapt, I die. Adapting is how I can navigate the waters of uncertainty and build the courage to turn challenges into opportunities. Adapting is seeking knowledge and always learning from those who seek to support and help me grow, using any resources available to have the best chance to survive. I use this water-filled layer as my courage to adapt, grow, and confront the obstacles of self-doubt.

WHAT DO YOU MEAN, "IF?"

———

IN THE SUMMER OF 1997, MY FAMILY MOVED TO
Denver, Colorado. Someone had convinced my oldest
brother that it would be easier to get a job there, and the
human services were better. We packed our apartment
into a U-Haul and drove all the way to Denver, Colorado.
It turned out everything was much more challenging in
Denver. The whole ordeal lasted two weeks. We came back
to Oregon faster than when we left.

When we got back to Beaverton, my mother cried for
weeks over the wrong decision that left us damn near
homeless. Our family friend, Haji Hasson, became our
hero and saved us from sleeping in the car or out in the
street. He was a Persian man who had lived in the US
since the '80s. He started the small local Mosque for the
small Muslim community in Beaverton during the '90s
and owned a Teriyaki restaurant. It was the only Halal

food in the area. The restaurant had an attic big enough to use as a bedroom and a small living space. When he heard we were coming back and had no place to stay, Haji offered his space above the restaurant. My brothers stayed with some friends and my mother, father, Mohammed, Heba, Zainab, and I squeezed into the attic.

I knew, even as a little kid, that we were financially at the bottom of the barrel. My older brothers tried to get their jobs back or get a new job. They apartment-hunted for weeks. Finally, Haji cosigned on a three-bedroom apartment where we could all move to. The apartment was small, with all nine of us together. It was OK, though. It finally felt normal again to be able to see everyone daily. It reminded me of when we lived together in the camp. Haji Hassan became an even closer friend to the family. He stopped by to check in and made sure we had enough food and whatever else we needed. My family struggled for the next few months, but we got back on our feet. My brothers made their way back into work, and things became a bit more settled.

By seventh grade, my English had gotten better, and I could finally speak comfortably. Though I made friends, I was still shy around girls and did my best to fit in and not stand out too much. I hung out a lot with the ESL crowd, a group of kids with many cultural backgrounds. We were all learning to speak, read, and write English as fast as we could to catch up with the other students. Though I picked up speaking pretty fast, reading and writing didn't come as easily.

My seventh-grade ESL teacher was harsh and demanded a lot from us. Many kids hardly understood what she was saying. During one of our class lessons, we discussed what we hoped to do after we graduated. She pulled up the giant poster filled with pictures of people doing random jobs and started to call on students.

"Alejandro, what are you going to do when you get to college?" she asked.

"I like cars, so, um, I want to be a mechanic or something car-related," my friend Alejandro said.

"That's good, but I don't even think you need college for that," Mrs. Carrie replied. "Olivia! What are you going to do when you get to college?"

"I want to become a nurse," Olivia replied, pointing to a picture of a nurse.

"You have to study a lot to be a nurse." She then stared in my direction.

"Hussein! What are you going to do if you get into college?"

"What do you mean, *if*? I'm going to college, and I'm going to get an architecture degree," I said. Mrs. Carrie cracked a laugh.

"That's one of the hardest degrees out there. I had friends who tried back when I was in college, and they all dropped out because it was so hard."

"I'm going to try."

"OK, good luck with that." Her voice of doubt roamed in my mind for the rest of the day. I realized, in that moment, that others may try to get you to believe you have a limitation, but the reality is, only you know what's possible for you. If I can survive a war and a refugee camp, I can get through architecture school.

I hated asking my mom and dad for money. They never had a lot, and I knew how much we'd struggled in the past. I tried to save some of my earnings to help with school supplies when we got back to school. But my oldest sister found out about a church that helped with school supplies. We went the next morning, a week before school, and stood in line. It felt great to get something I needed donated and given to me.

When the eighth grade started, I was ready to get focused and do better than the year before. I got to meet my new

ESL teacher, Selena. She was young, vibrant, and had a very uplifting attitude, always smiling and positive. Selena helped me recognize that I, too, had powers to do what I wanted. She helped me get out of ESL and into mainstream classes. She knew I was ready and pushed me to get after it. She saw more potential in me than I could see in myself.

Most of my friends were students of color from all kinds of backgrounds. I loved being around so many different languages and kids from different parts of the world. We were all different and unique but still trying very hard to fit into American culture. As we wrapped up middle school, I passed my ESL test to get out of the program. I felt like I was on top of the world.

Three years later, I had completely forgotten about the book I wrote and illustrated in fifth grade. I got called out of class because there was a package at the front office for me. I was a little nervous. I had no idea who would send me a package. When I opened it, my eyes lit up with excitement. It was my book! I had ranked in the top 200 out of 200,000 participants nationwide. I couldn't believe it. I was impatient all day to run home and show my mom and dad that I got an award and my book returned to me. They hugged me and congratulated me and asked if I was going to make more books.

I shrugged it off and said, "Inshallah," which means "God

willing." Writing another book didn't seem as "cool" as what I was doing. You know, trying to fit in.

THE FRESH PRINCE
OF BEAVERTON

———

EVERYTHING SHOVED INTO MOTION AS I STEPPED into my teenage years. My father became strict about who I hung out with and for how long, always giving me advice on not slipping up or being swayed by the "American lifestyle." I had to balance who I was at home with who I was at school. I was a kid from Iraq, an artist, and a refugee, but I kept all that stuff buried inside. I couldn't be one person.

On my first day of freshman orientation, I sat as high as I could in the bleachers. A kid with a huge afro came up the steps and sat next to me.

"Yo, what up? I'm Nick, that's a fresh Hugo Boss polo. Where you get that at?"

"I got it from my brother, man; it's a pass-me-down."

We both chuckled. He said his jeans and shirt were his brother's, too. We started to talk about fashion and sports.

"You play ball?"

"I mean, I hoop a little on the streets but not a team or anything."

"Well, you should try out, man, and get on the squad."

Nick was one of the coolest kids I met. He was funny, loud, confident, and crazy smart. A class clown and a great basketball player and super intelligent. You either loved him or avoided him so the jokes didn't come flying your way. No matter what, he was always Nick. Some of my friends made it look easy—school, fitting in and just being youthful seemed so easy.

It was different for me. I struggled to make sense of my identity as a Middle Eastern kid. I took all kinds of classes and maintained good grades, but it felt like I was busting my ass to keep up with everything. By the time I got home, I was exhausted, and I still had to start my homework or study for the next thing.

My parents demanded good grades and for me not to mess

up the opportunity to go to college. They wanted me to be an engineer or an architect, and fun was not a part of the equation. Many times, I had the bad habit of lying to my parents about where I was going. Being a typical teenager, having a social life felt important.

Most of my friends didn't have a curfew. I had to be home by nine o'clock in the evening at the absolute latest. In my mind, I needed to show my friends that I was a normal American kid like they were—that I also was going to get a car, that I could have a girlfriend, and get a good job. I wanted to fit in, so I talked, walked, and dressed like most of my peers at school. By my sophomore year, I started to get the hang of keeping up the facade. I was one Hussein at school, and another Hussein at home. It felt like I was keeping a big secret from everyone.

I was one of very few Middle Eastern kids in my entire school, and I didn't fall into any specific crew. I kept the right balance and never got too cliquey with one group or another. I started listening to a lot of hip-hop and rap. Tupac Shakur, Biggie, Nas, Lauren Hill, Jay-Z, and not to mention Outkast and The Fugees! The rhyming flow, mixed with storytelling, was so creative. I loved that hip-hop spoke about the struggle. I connected to that. The rhymes reminded me so much of the poetry nights my father would host over dinners in the camp. Spoken word and storytelling is the essence of capturing attention, put that with music and it's like honey for the ears.

Hip-hop tells such a vivid story of working hard for your dreams; in 2Pac's "Changes," I would listen to his voice so deep that it would make me cry and wonder if a change would ever come. "Dear Mama" is one of my favorite songs from 2Pac. It made me cry thinking of how much my mother sacrificed for my brothers and me. I knew I wanted to make my own mother and father proud and do good in the world through art and architecture one day. I had an urge to self-express my outsider perspective; however, I didn't know how to use my gifts and artistic abilities to say something about my perspective. Though I wasn't from the ghetto and wasn't nearly as poor as these rappers depicted their early childhoods, I was from a refugee camp; we didn't have faucets or electricity for years. I could relate on a deep level, yet I was too embarrassed to tell anyone I was actually from a refugee camp. My family was on welfare, and fear of judgment began to be real. I, too, had dreams of money never being an issue, or that I would own a business someday.

I watched "The Fresh Prince of Bel-Air" on repeat. I didn't live in Beverly Hills, but living in an apartment in Oregon was way better than a tent in a refugee camp in the middle of the desert. Watching Will Smith's character deal with a different environment through comedy always helped uplift me. Much like the show, our family drama was always unfolding. But unlike the show, it wasn't always funny.

Growing up in our house was chaotic. The family drama varied day to day and week to week. There would be a few yelling matches between my older siblings, over a town-car service they tried to start. My brothers struggled with work and life just as much as I did. My brothers switched jobs every few months or so, trying to make ends meet. My oldest brother found what he was good at—selling cars. The other started truck driving. I took a weekend job serving gyros at the Saturday Market in Portland.

Everyone struggled financially. Our unresolved trauma from the refugee camp poured out in ways that were tough to handle. My mother and father held on to traditional ways of thinking, which was a gift and a curse. Being protective meant we needed to ask for permission to do just about anything, like going to the movies or playing basketball outside with some neighborhood friends.

The Al-Jazeera and other Arabic news channels were always on TV in the living room, full of the horrific tragedies that continued to plague the Middle East. There was never ease; I felt like I always needed to be anxious about something. Whether it was my grades, trying to fit in, or making sure I went with my mother or father to their next doctor's appointment to translate. I often hid in my room, praying for it to be over.

It became increasingly difficult for my mother to connect to her children, especially her sons. She became like a supercomputer and documented a constant series of past experiences in her head she couldn't forget. These grievances came up on many occasions when something was said and perceived in the wrong way. She began to feel as if her sons and daughters were drifting away. Being such a tight-knit family before, it was easier to feel a sense of control by knowing the ins and outs of each of our lives. She felt disconnected from us, not speaking the language and staying a house mom. Adding on medical conditions such as diabetes made life even more difficult.

Everything seemed great on the surface. I learned to mask my growing pains, insecurities, family drama, and endless madness. I knew I didn't have a bad life, but I wanted to be more like my American friends who didn't have the same worries.

* * *

My father had different worries and was strict around what he allowed, especially for my younger sister and me. He was always reminding me that while I lived in America, I shouldn't become an American. "I don't want you to lose your religion and culture," he warned. "Yes, Baba, Inshallah, I won't," I replied. I couldn't distinguish religion from culture: the two were the same to me. My father's biggest pain and stress came from raising his kids in a foreign land that would delete who they were, and that we would leave Islam altogether. Being a religious man, his fear was us leaving our faith and disconnecting from our heritage.

I learned many lessons from my father about the role of the Quran in everyday life. For him, praying was an ingrained habit. No matter what was happening around him, his anchor was the praying mat three times a day. In the morning before sunrise, I would hear him prepping for prayer. I would be getting ready to get to the bus stop to go to school. At times, he invited me to join, encouraging me that it would help the day be great. I actually did feel good on the days I joined him in prayer. He had a way of setting an example for prayer and all of the other Islamic duties.

Going to the Mosque, reading the Quran, and practicing prayer was crucial to my growth. No one was going to teach me Islam at school, so my father needed to constantly make space for it in my life. He never made me do anything or even punished me, he simply tried to explain the benefits of sacred tasks such as prayer, listening to the Quran, giving to charity, and fasting. The Arabic audio versions of the Quran were beautiful and poetic. This was a beautiful part of my morning routine. When I listened to them, I felt calmer and in touch with a higher power at play.

In my high school, I was one of only two kids that observed Ramadan. The religious celebration was hardly taught in school. Many of my classmates would call me crazy or say that I was lying and drinking water when no one was looking. Some even tried to tempt me into having a bite of their burger, pizza, or salad. I would resist every time. I had been practicing this resistance since I was in the refugee camp. Fasting isn't about what you resist: it is more about what you gain.

Most people think Ramadan is about only fasting from food, but it's much more intense than that. You have to really commit. Not eating is hard, but not drinking any fluids all day is even harder. There's also no sex, cursing, or talking bad about others, or spreading rumors.

The month functions like a reset button. Until Ramadan, I don't notice how much my body is operating on autopilot. The first week is usually the hardest, as my body has to adjust to not having water and food from sunrise to sunset. After the first week, though, I feel much stronger. If I can refrain from eating and drinking, I can conquer anything. It's more than that, of course—it's about my ability to control my habits. It gives my mind and body time to heal and clean up the inside. I question my actions and thoughts and become more aware of my attention.

I was not anywhere near perfect, but I tried. Sometimes when the day got tough, I broke my fast midday, buckling under the pressure of school. But there is a certain pleasure in trying and knowing things won't always go as planned.

Each night, an hour before the sun waves goodbye, my family would gather to talk, pray, and get ready to eat. When you have been fasting all day, any food or beverage is worth gold. The smell alone was like heaven. I never appreciate food and water more than when I don't put it in my body for an entire day.

The beef kafta and chicken shish kebabs sizzled as they came out of the oven. They were the centerpiece. Salads, pita bread, and lentil soups with dates covered the rest of the mat. My father started the meal with a prayer. He recited Surah Al-Fatiha from the Quran and dedicated it to his parents and my mom's parents. He repeated it and prayed that Allah eases the pain and suffering of all who are going through tough times. "Bismillah al Rahman al Raheem"—In the name of Allah, the most beneficent, the merciful.

We sat on the ground together, breaking bread and passing the food around. When I fast, my stomach seems to shrink. After about fifteen minutes of eating a little of this and a lot of that, everyone was full. My mom made plates from the leftovers for our neighbors and asked me to deliver them.

Whether we broke our fast at four o'clock in the afternoon for a winter sunset, or ten o'clock in the evening in the summer, when the sun never wants to set, we kept close to our traditions. My father would spend tons of time reading the Quran, praying, and sharing his wisdom. I loved those days. I always felt the love roaming around our house.

MY SIDE OF THE STORY

——

ON THE MORNING OF SEPTEMBER 11, 2001, I WALKED to the bus stop and greeted my main homies, Adam and Hector. They were both talking about how a plane hit the World Trade Center in New York.

"Wait, what?" I asked.

"Yes, man, a plane crashed into the tower!" Hector said.

"Did they lose control?"

"I don't know, man. It may have been intentional."

I remember not believing something that crazy could happen in New York.

The bus picked us up, and we headed to school. By the

time we got to school, the situation had intensified. Everyone was talking about the two planes. I was so confused about what was happening.

As the day went on, the drama continued. Every classroom had a television on. We all sat observing the news. From one teacher to the next, the news evolved of what they now were calling a "terrorist attack." The people behind it were Arab Muslims from the Middle East.

The pictures of the "Ahmeds" and "Mohammeds" on the screen looked like me. They had names that were close to mine and my brothers'. A rush of emotions coursed through my body.

When the school day ended, I got on the bus and my homies began to look at me funny, saying things like, "Yo, HUSSEIN! Why are your people attacking us and killing us?"

"Man, get out of here! Those are not my people," I said. "I know them as much as you!"

I got home and finally got to talk with my family. "What is happening, Baba?" I asked.

"I have no idea," my father said. "I guess they are Saudis or from Afghanistan. These people are crazy, and this has nothing to do with who we are."

My father made sure I understood that this was not how we express Islam to the world. "Be patient," he urged. "There is always more to the story, and soon it will reveal itself."

We all sat around watching clip after clip of the planes hitting the towers in slow-motion, crashing down as they imploded on themselves. It was something out of a movie. I was so sad for all the men and women who died during this horrific act.

The next few months in school were awful. Let racism begin and have no mercy. Students around me started to distance themselves. If I didn't feel it before, I now felt it like hot coals. Cowards whispered, "Sand nigga," or "Fuck your people," when I walked by. I tried to pretend I didn't hear them.

When I was sitting in class, hoping the day would end, a heated debate sparked with another student. "Why do your people hate America so much?" he asked.

"Why am I a spokesperson for terrorism?" I asked. "They are not 'my people.' But the US has been at war with so much of the Middle East since World War II. Wars break out and then they place puppet dictators into these countries, who rule with an iron fist and dehumanize the people and create poverty. No one says anything about that. I'm not justifying the actions of these terrorists, just showing how the US isn't exactly an angel either."

I tried to end that debate and stopped talking altogether.

The next day at school, when I was walking to English class, I saw two guys standing in the hallway around the corner. I said, "Yo, what up."

"Don't 'what up' me, you Osama Bin Laden looking moth-erfucker!" one of the guys said.

I turned to look at his face to see if he was joking or serious.

He got into my face and repeated, "DON'T 'WHAT UP' ME, YOU OSAMA BIN LADEN LOOKING MOTHER FUCKER!"

My all-time lowest moment was when I gave in to what happened next. I felt the accumulation of all the negative shit, racial jokes, and whispers. I grabbed his collar and pulled his face in, punching him with my right hook. No warning, no pushing. I blacked out and lost control.

I got pulled off by one of the football coaches. I finally looked up and realized half of his class was surrounding us.

I had never been pulled into the counselor's office. Here,

I waited for my father to pick me up, embarrassed, frustrated, and still angry. My entire time in school in America, I had been called every name in the book. I couldn't hold my punches back anymore. I would not give the kid or anyone else permission to label me. I wasn't sorry, and if punishment meant that others wouldn't say anything to me again, so be it.

When my father came to pick me up, all he could say was that he was sorry for my actions. The assistant principal gave me a three-day suspension. My father only asked if the kid was OK. "I don't condone my son's actions," my father said. "But I can understand his anger." He knew I had to stand up for myself.

On our way home, my father asked if I was OK. I told him through tears that these kids wouldn't stop. I had to do what I had to do.

"That's life, son," he said. "People, situations, and an endless array of negativity will always come our way. We are defined by how we respond to these situations."

I was too upset even to process his wisdom, but I knew he was right. I had the next few days to reflect on the whole situation. My journey of overcoming more barriers was far from over.

When I came back to school, I ignored the chatter and

was very focused. I wanted to finish high school strong and go on to college.

* * *

In my junior year of high school, I took a writing class with Mrs. Trudell. She was no joke, she pushed us hard to tell our emotions through story. She demanded that we work hard; she wasn't going to be giving out free passing grades. It seemed no one could impress her. More than half of my assignments came back lacking. From grammar to not-deep-enough descriptions of emotions or character. I knew I had to commit to her class assignments. I struggled with taking tests; I was always looking for classes that didn't have too many quizzes and tests. Her class was all about reading and doing writing assignments. With that weight off my shoulders, I could focus on what she was trying to teach.

Our final assignment was to write an eight-page essay on pretty much anything we wanted. The only requirements were that it needed to be in a story format, and it needed to be true. All the other assignments had been leading up to this. I knew it was time to share my life story and how I came to be in her class.

I wrote how we fled Iraq and lost everything. I wrote about my father's pain and art to rescue us from the desert camp.

I wrote painful memories of being on welfare. I wrote my September 11, 2001, experience and how I encouraged people to be aware of another perspective.

I filled up ten pages with ease.

I felt such a sense of release. I had been holding so much back. It felt good to write something real and share who I really was. I turned my paper in and prayed to Allah that I would get a good grade to pass her class and move on.

A week later, Mrs. Trudell got through grading our papers. Something was a bit different. I could feel it as soon as I walked into the classroom.

"I read your paper twice last night," she told me. "I had no idea."

"It was that bad?" I asked. "Please let me rewrite it."

She laughed as her eyes watered up. She asked if I would read my story aloud to the class. "It's something we all need to hear right now."

My palms started to become sweaty. I was nervous that my classmates were going to laugh at me but also excited that my story mattered in a time when people needed a different perspective. It was the same excitement I felt when I submitted my book in that contest when I was younger.

With ten minutes left in class, Mrs. Trudell announced to the other students that I would read my paper out loud. They didn't seem impressed or even care. As I walked up to the front of the class, I became even more nervous. After I finished reading, I finally looked up to make eye contact with the students. Most of them were on the edge of the seat, and Mrs. Trudell was nodding her head with tears in her eyes.

After class, I thanked Mrs. Trudell for letting me tell my story. I felt great sharing who I was and not what the media made me out to be. She suggested that I keep writing. I had a lot to say, and I needed to channel it into creative writing and art.

After the rush of telling my story through writing and doing a mini-speech, Mrs. Trudell insisted that I take a speech class. Learning how to express oneself verbally was something I had taken for granted up until that point. My speech class was another stepping-stone towards feeling comfortable. I had found yet another powerful way to express who I was.

Mrs. Hayes, my teacher, spoke with a thick southern accent.

"Everyone starts at a passing grade. It's your job to keep your passing grade," she said.

She was tough and not afraid to put us on the spot in front of the class. She was trying to make it close to a real-life experience. I loved her teaching style. She taught us about different speakers who changed the way we see the world through the spoken word. I was inspired and intrigued, as most of them had rough upbringings.

The final assignment was a six-minute speech on pretty much anything. I decided to do what works for me—my personal story, from Iraq to how I got where I'm standing. If I applied speaking techniques to my story, I knew I could get more emotions across. I could hear her pieces of wisdom in my head while I wrote down my speech. "Put humor in like salt and pepper," she told us. "Be yourself throughout the story; it's the best way to connect with the audience."

Practicing and fitting my story into six minutes was essential. I used all the techniques we had learned in class, like how to structure your speaking pattern, making it useful and purposeful. I practiced in front of the mirror in my room over and over again. I maintained my smile, made eye contact, and spoke with my head held high and my shoulders pushed back. I had something positive to say, and that required confidence.

By the day of the presentation, I knew my speech well; I didn't need note cards. I was dressed up with a button-down and slacks and I had combed my hair.

"Hussein! Are you ready?" she asked.

As I stood up, I could hear her voice in my head. "Have CONFIDENCE." I braced myself and pumped out my chest. I walked with intention to the front of the class.

"I need you to listen and feel the story I am about to tell you," I said. "Imagine living in the middle of the desert, with nothing but a sheet of canvas in between you and all the elements."

All the students sat up in their seats. "Imagine being thirsty for days on end." I went on and told my story with passion, using long pauses to let parts sink in. I nailed the timing. It felt like a ton of bricks lifted off my shoulders, being able to share my story. I had kept myself hidden for so long, thinking my life as a refugee was the wrong part of who I was.

LAYER 6

FOCUSED
FLEXIBILITIES

SITTING A FEW FEET BEHIND MY FATHER, I WATCHED as he painted, mixing colors, dipping the brush in blobs of oil paint, and applying them to the canvas. I watched this happen for hours. I observed and tried to focus on the task he gave me for the day. He handed me one colored pencil, the red one, and five sheets of paper.

"Hussein Habibi, I want you to draw this cup and this pillow. Use only the red pencil until you can't hold it anymore from sharpening it." I went to work, sketched, colored, faded the objects from every angle. I sketched all afternoon and wore down that colored pencil to a nub. I was able to focus and hone in on my task.

"Hussein, here's the color blue; look around for anything blue in our tent. Tell me what's blue?"

"The blanket, the tube of paint, the basket," I replied.

"Good, I want you to lay them out and draw them."

I sketched them all and detailed every square millimeter of that tube of paint and basket with the blue colored pencil.

I made lots of mistakes, drawing outside the lines that I sketched, messing up small details, and tearing the paper up. At times I got frustrated and crumpled the paper up because I couldn't get what was in front of me to look right.

"Try again, Hussein. Don't let this upset you; allow it to calm you."

I tried over and over again until the objects came to life on my paper.

"Hussein, you have to be focused, but allow for the flexibility to make mistakes. Mistakes are a part of the process, and the act of trying is the practice that helps you get more focused and clear on your art."

Two years after this process went on, my father finally gave me a full set of colored pencils. At first, I was afraid to use them all.

I froze, staring at my paper, not knowing what to draw. After hours of staring into the abyss of white paper, my father said, "It's OK. When we have too many options, we all get scared to try. Use your fear, face the paper, and tell it what you want to say."

I wrote in Arabic, "I'm going to save you."

He smiled. "Show me how you will save us."

I drew a little boy with a garbage-bag cape tied to his neck, holding hands with other people and flying away.

I learned to show the blank paper what I wanted to say. I learned color theory very young; more importantly, I learned focus comes from indulging in the process. Mistakes seldom define the result; the flexibility and willingness to use the mistakes as leverage lead to a more valuable experience.

This layer is full of shelves and racks that hold all types of previous practice, from muscle memories to ideas not fully drawn out. This layer is pivotal for the experience of what I have tried and failed at. Failing isn't bad or negative; it's necessary to improve what I'm trying to be good at. It's the layer where everything is documented for my review and to learn from for my next mission.

TOO SCARED TO TRY

———

IN MY JUNIOR YEAR OF HIGH SCHOOL, I DECIDED TO go to Portland Community College. I had heard that community college didn't need more than a simple test to get in, and I was too afraid to take the SATs.

When the last term of my senior year came around, it was too late even to try. In our final assembly, I sat high up in the bleachers watching the gym full of students. The principal stood at the lectern congratulating and announcing all of the students who earned scholarships. So many people I knew stood up as we clapped for them. They had won thousands of dollars to attend some excellent universities. I knew how much hard work went into earning scholarships. I commended them, but I started wondering what I had done wrong.

"What have I been doing the last four years of my life!?" I

wondered to myself. Most of my close friends were athletes; they, too, had scholarships to play sports in college. I missed the whole point. I had wasted the last four years being too scared to try.

It was my fault. I didn't apply myself as much as I could have. I was not in any after-school programs. I wasn't in any leadership positions. I hadn't taken art classes because I thought I was too good for them. I was average at best. I had passed my classes. But beyond that, my fear had given me endless reasons as to why I shouldn't try. I had used the excuse that I was not smart enough or good enough. I didn't take the time to research or even ask for help.

My parents didn't know much about the school system. They assumed everyone went to the same universities. In Iraq, there are a handful of universities and types of schools; you sort of choose your path and try to get into the school. If accepted, great; if not, you went to the military. They had no idea what scholarships were and how to get them. I knew other kids had parents who pushed them to do all these extracurriculars. But the excuses ran out. If I kept blaming my current predicament on where I was from, or what my parents could do for me, it would continue to limit my growth.

That summer, I was in more emotional pain than I could bear. I knew if I had applied myself, I could do the things that most of these kids were able to do. I needed to ask more questions, be bold, and go after what I wanted.

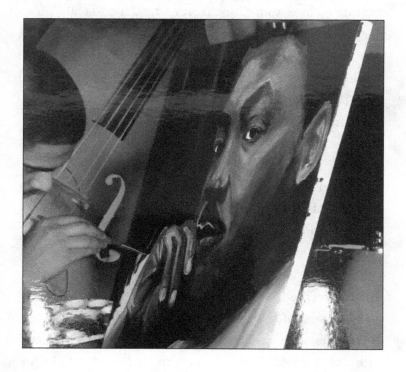

I decided to try to get into Portland State University (PSU) to study architecture. My sister Zainab had been at the school for a few years. She came to my rescue and told me I needed to take an exam to gain entry.

"Allah, help me through this test," I prayed. I tried my best. The results didn't show up after a few weeks. I started to lose hope. I assumed I didn't pass. I decided it was time to apply to Portland Community College, where I would go first and later try to transfer to PSU for architecture. I talked myself into the easy route. On my way to the community college, something inside urged me to call PSU.

The woman on the line helped pull up my record. "We mailed out the results a few weeks ago, but it seems we have the wrong address for you." She told me I had done well on the test and could sign up for classes for the fall term.

I dropped the phone and yelled, "YES, YES! I got in. I'm in! I did it!" I called my parents right away and told them the news. I called my sister and told her how grateful I was for her help.

To get accepted into the architecture program, I needed to take a year of beginner classes. After my freshman year, I would be able to submit a portfolio of my work to get into the program. I had been claiming I wanted to be an architect for so long. I was ready to finally start.

* * *

College is not cheap; living isn't either. I waited for my quarterly financial aid check to show up, so I could buy the oldest textbooks for classes. I had gotten a job my last year of high school working at a bowling alley, earning $250 a week. It was something but not enough. I needed to earn some real money for day-to-day living. I'm a creative kid, and I grew up working side hustles.

At the bowling alley, I got to work at the front desk and at times I worked with Terry, the owner. He knew everybody in the bowling industry. I learned so much about business and customer service from him. We always had great conversations on life, school, and adventures. I always asked about how he was able to build his business and grow the bowling alley. He always referred to reading and enjoying what you do. He loved bowling, he loved the environment and the people. I appreciated his wisdom, and during one conversation, he said, "When you get a chance, go get the book *Rich Dad Poor Dad*. It's a great book; you will love it."

I went to the Beaverton library the next day and checked out the book. By the time I finished it that week, my perspective on the idea of work had changed. The ideas were simple yet challenging to put into practice. Success, I learned, is a series of habits, not a destination or a pot of gold at the end. A lot of what I read were things Terry was practicing. I was very much intrigued with figuring out how to find a way to leverage my talents. Figuring out what I loved and how I could use it to earn money and connect with people.

The next day, I drew a picture of Jay-Z from his new album cover with a pencil and a Sharpie. I asked my boy Brandon to come with me to the Beaverton Mall to heat press some T-shirts. When we went to pick them up, they were small on the chest and didn't look good at all.

"Why don't you paint it directly on the T-shirts?" Brandon offered.

"I guess I can do that," I said. "It'll take much longer."

"Exactly. They will be like art pieces," he said.

"I like the way you think, Brandon." I realized a hand-painted T-shirt could be more valuable. I'd seen the air-brushed look that artists used to do at the markets I used to work at. I hadn't seen too many people actually hand paint a T-shirt before.

This was my turning point. Realizing that I could do this, and others believed in me, gave me the extra push I needed.

I went to the craft store and got some blank white T-shirts and ink to work on a project. I had watched guys at Saturday Market spray paint T-shirts and sell them for thirty dollars. I knew I could do that and sell them on eBay. Something deep inside told me that it wouldn't hurt to just try it.

When I got home, I cleaned off my desk, and set the T-shirt

on the table. I googled an image of Jay-Z's new album. It's a silhouette of him holding the brim of his hat facing out. I sketched it out on the T-shirt and began to paint.

After an hour, I took a step back and looked at the shirt. I felt a rush through my body! The next day, I brought it over to Brandon's house and held it up in his face. "What do you think, bro?"

"Oh my God, that's fresh. I need that right now."

I started hand-painting T-shirts of Michael Jordan and other athletes that I sold on eBay, earning fifty to seventy-five dollars per shirt. I loved it.

The word started to get out. From being on campus, I got to know tons of people in student groups that needed T-shirts. I would spend up to four to six hours a day hand-painting orders for friends and people online. I created a part-time job for myself, practicing painting and creating T-shirts. These T-shirts took up a lot of time, but the income was essential for me to live on while I went to college. The hustle combined doing what I love, using my talents, and flexibility around my class schedule. I earned more painting T-shirts in a week than any other job I had ever had.

Eventually, I started outgrowing my hand-painting operation and looked for ways to make production faster. I started to watch YouTube videos about the screen-printing process and met a local guy who owned a screen-printing company that printed for businesses around town.

When I visited his shop, I saw the presses and heaters humming. T-shirt after T-shirt came out of a conveyor belt. I knew where my T-shirt operation needed to go, and I had to understand the technique. I asked if he could give me pointers on the printing process. The first time I pulled a squeegee across a screen, making my first print on a T-shirt, my eyes lit up. My brain started firing up ideas about starting my own T-shirt company. I wanted to design a line of T-shirts that had positive, conscious messaging. I offered to sweep his shop and help fold T-shirts while I learned the craft. I worked for him for free for months to learn the craft as best I could.

After a few months, I was able to get the hang of it. I became fascinated with owning my own little print studio. I used $800 from my financial aid check to buy a simple four-color press from eBay and some ink and squeegees.

But doing everything out of my room was not workable. I needed to rent a space to use as a studio. I told my friend Patrick, who owned a barbershop close to campus. He offered me the basement of his barbershop and said he would charge me only when I started to earn money. The space was a mess, but I saw tons of potential. It was in a prime location, close to school. I moved in and cleaned it up, painting the walls, building a rack for my supplies, and putting down plastic tiles. I turned an old bathtub into my screen wash station and made a light table to expose the screens and bring my designs to life.

Two weeks later, I was ready for business. I spent most evenings at my print shop, working on screen printing jobs, or doing projects for my architecture studio classes. My sleep schedule was way off. While the orders kept flowing, I worked very hard to keep my grades up and stay active in classes.

LOSING SIGHT

———

I NEEDED TO CREATE A PORTFOLIO TO GET INTO THE architecture program. Many students apply every year, and only about fifty get accepted. But my portfolio was the last thing on my mind. I was too busy trying to earn money to pay my bills. I was so focused on what was right in front of me, I forgot about the whole picture.

By the end of the school year, things got intense. My stress was mounting about urgent screen-printing jobs and hustling to photograph my work. Developing an architecture portfolio last minute is not a good idea, but I procrastinated until the end.

A week before it was due, my imposter syndrome started kicking in, the same one I felt entering my first classroom all those years ago in the refugee camp and then again when I started school in America. What if I'm not good enough for this? What if I don't get accepted? What if I do, and I can't pay for it? I couldn't sleep anymore, knowing that I had put off the most crucial project of my college career. I considered not even turning one in.

With only a few days left, I sat down and worked on my portfolio late into the morning. I had no idea what I was doing. I pulled together images, sketches, and models from all my classes the previous year. I put together a book using Photoshop to lay out the pages. I tried to play it safe and make it straightforward, but my lack of expertise and unfamiliarity with the design program were a terrible combination.

After a few all-nighters and tons of Red Bull, I was still not done. At one in the afternoon the day it was due, I rushed to get it printed. Waiting in line at FedEx, my heart was beating out of my chest. When they finished printing and binding the portfolio, I flipped through it for the first time. It looked terrible. Something was off, but I had no choice. I had to turn something in.

At 4:40 in the afternoon, I sped on the 217 Freeway to get from Beaverton to Portland by five o'clock in the evening on a Friday. By some miracle, traffic wasn't thick. I zoomed past cars with all my intention of making it. As I parked, I saw people I knew walking out.

I ran to the front door, but it was locked. It was 5:04. A few others ran up and felt the same heart-dropping feeling.

I was so down and drained. I knew exactly what I had done wrong. Too many distractions! I had messed around too much with T-shirts and wasted precious time. I walked back to my car, threw down the portfolio on the passenger seat, and asked myself, "What am I going to do now?"

I figured that was it. I was done with architecture. It was time to do something else.

My dad asked if I could retake the classes or try again next month. I told him that's not how it works. I couldn't apply; I had missed the deadline. I needed to retake a few courses and re-apply with another portfolio next year in time for submissions. I knew what I had to do. I wasn't sure if it was worth the pain again. I wanted this; I wanted this to prove to my father, brothers, sisters, and my mother that all of the hard work they put in to ensure I got a good education was worth it. I knew what I had to do. I knew I had to try again.

I could see that look of disappointment in his eyes. At first, he didn't reply. He took a deep breath, and said, "You have a plan, I have a plan, but Allah has the ultimate plan."

LAYER 7

PURPOSE COMPASS

AT THE CAMP, MY FAMILY AND I LAID DOWN ON A blanket right after dinner one cool summer evening. The sky was beautiful and clear, the stars illuminated the darkness, and the Milky Way stretched from one end of my sight to the other. I slowly dozed off listening to my father's stories of our ancestors and how they used to navigate the empty deserts from one oasis to another until they made it from the holy city of Mecca to the holy city of Karbala where Imam Hussein, the grandson of the Prophet Mohammed, died fighting to keep Islam alive.

My father looked up to the heavens above and poetically spoke words I could never forget.

"Our purpose and life are written in the patterns of stars; we carry the missions of those who left us the light to guide our path. We need knowledge like sand needs this desert. We must seek the inner bravery to tame lions, though we are wanderers of the desert. Our inner compass guides us like a camel to an oasis, the water of which quenches our thirst for knowledge and further guides us through but never around our deepest fears."

This layer is a metaphor for a compass, much like an astrolabe used in the ancient days of the Golden Age of Islam, showing time, location, and other components to understand where you are about the heavens above you. People tend to look outside of themselves for a purpose they long for when, in reality, we are the purpose. Our gifts are the tools that bring our purpose out into the world through various artistic expressions.

The key, however, is that every purpose is service. Once we can fully understand ourselves, our talents, and our human abilities, we can use them for something outside of ourselves. The meaning of your purpose is woven through a lived experience. The purpose then continues the behavior of a compass guiding us from one mission to the next, one person or project to the next, until we meet our resolve.

THE PROCESS IS THE GOAL

———

AFTER MY SECOND YEAR OF COLLEGE, I DECIDED TO PUT aside all my distractions and took a long break from screen-printing T-shirts in the basement. I borrowed $1,500 from my brothers so that I could focus exclusively on school.

With the guidance of some friends who made it into the program years prior, I remade my architecture portfolio. I turned it in on time and was ready to receive my acceptance letter. A week before the summer semester, I got my letter. My stomach sank. I didn't get accepted again; they noted that taking a summer class would help and that I would have another chance to submit at the end of the summer.

I was used to rejections now. I was going to try again and pour everything into the summer class. I started working night and day, recreating some of my old work and putting in new work, adding more style and story. I put my pride aside and kept chipping more off my ego, asking professors how I could improve my portfolio. I got a lot of advice, which helped me understand the process more. I made some great friends during the summer class and felt a sense of fulfillment and community, feeling like I belonged.

In my third attempt to get into the program, I finished and printed my portfolio a week before it was due. I was proud of my work and ready. A week later, I got my letter of acceptance. The hard work and support paid off. I shared the news with my parents, and they were so excited. My mom cooked up all my favorites and invited the family to come and celebrate.

The architecture program was intense but so satisfying. Hands-on creative learning requires you to put in hours every day to get ideas out. During my studio classes, the process was as necessary as the result. Failing was how I got better for the next project. I learned how to sketch, maintain a daily journal, photograph and document every sketch model, every plan and sectional drawing. I did endless perspective drawings, light studies, and scanned everything I did; I learned the art of the process. Documentation is just as important to the process as the actual end product. I realized this is the "show your work" to solving a math problem. It is the way to convey thoughts in form; I was addicted to ensuring every step of my thinking was on paper.

The process was the story on which I could lean to ensure that my critiques showed my thinking process and how I arrived at final design decisions. Reading architecture books formulated a deeper theoretical meaning of architecture. From Steven Holl, who used light to redefine what it means to be in a space, to Ando, a Japanese architect who taught me about concrete and how to use it with elegance. I appreciated the process; I fell in love with learning about how the architect brings to life concepts through materials, which speak and convey emotions. Materials are to architects what words are to a poet.

I studied my ancestors' architecture forms from the development of arches, domes, and creating cooling systems in the desert through fountains and courtyards. Mud huts to mosques, and now the development of skyscrapers to make a statement to the world. I sunk deep into the essence of architecture and learned the art of simplicity from Eastern perspective and the economics of building condos in the western world of what drives architecture. I hopped from one oasis of knowledge to the next, learning more with intention and further enriching my deep desire to become an architect.

Late in the evening around midnight, I was listening to 2Pac out of my computer when no one was around. I heard a voice come from the back: "Yo, turn that up."

I looked behind me, and this kid Max was nodding his head. He sat there, working away on his laptop. "Oh, you like 2Pac?"

"How can you not? He's like the greatest."

Max and I kept hustling all through architecture classes together. We stayed late and worked hard into the evening listening to tunes and crushing projects.

* * *

In my last year at architecture school, I was given the opportunity to travel to Ladakh, India, for a month to build parts of a school around a monastery. I wanted to go on this journey and travel to this beautiful place, tucked high in a Himalayan valley, where my dad once lived for a few years.

I wanted to see and learn from the culture, the people, the architecture, and the art—the whole thing. Living and eating in India was not expensive. I knew I could manage that. But I didn't have much money and was in dire need of a plane ticket.

I managed to pull funds together from my brothers and hopped on this journey to learn and explore. We landed in the smallest airport I have ever been to—a landing strip and a gas station that also acted as an airport. We got a bus to go into town and met some of the other cohorts.

I saw people from almost every faith living and working together. At the heart of town, a mosque was across from a Buddhist temple. It was a great reminder of how to live in peace. We made local friends, who treated us to bottomless tea, food, and fun gatherings. I learned so much from the locals about who they are and how to live a simple life. As they walked around, everyone seemed happy and was smiling. It made me realize how little you need to live a beautiful life. After a few weeks of living in Ladakh, I felt more at more peace than I had felt in a long time.

Coming back to the States, I had a new perspective on life from my experience. I realized my happiness comes from helping others in some way; service is something I love, and I uncovered it during this phenomenal trip.

* * *

In the summer of 2011, I graduated from college with precisely what I wanted—a degree in architecture. I'm not sure I would have been able to without the help and support of countless people behind me. I thought back to my seventh-grade teacher, who laughed when I said I wanted to study architecture.

To be able to say I finished the architecture program at Portland State University was a huge deal. I had given up endless parties, nights at clubs, and most of my social life to earn this piece of paper. Who would have thought a little boy from Iraq, kicking up dust with more obstacles than you could count, could achieve this? I did. It was in my gut the whole time. I had crushed every doubt I had about myself.

When I finally received my degree and went out in the real world, I worked briefly for one of my professors as an unpaid intern. I actually disliked the work more than I thought. Designing a bathroom for a super-privileged family for months and them not deciding on where to put a toilet blew my mind. I remembered the camp and when I used to go out in the middle of nowhere and just handle my business.

This specific job was simple. I knew what I was doing: draw up a plan, make some mockups, sell it to the client, get permits, get a contractor, get paid. However, this level of privilege opened up my eyes to a world I had no idea about. I wanted a way to use my expertise to build and make things that mattered for people who could really use my value for the good of the communities. For two months this indecisiveness went on about a toilet while I was broke, not getting paid, and the downturned economy squeezed the breath out of me.

The economy was on its knees during the 2011 recession, and it made it really difficult to obtain a job, especially in a field where many people were losing jobs. I tried for months to submit portfolios, take on internships or anything I could get my hands on. Nothing panned out and it was very frustrating.

I really wanted to explore my architectural ideas; however, the timing seemed off. I wanted to build libraries and mosques and figure out a way to help refugees. I couldn't connect the dots between where I was and where I wanted to be. Maybe this wasn't for me after all. I wasn't quite sure how to place it in a form yet. I felt like I just got through one door only to see many others closed. Confused at where I was standing, I needed to figure out what was next.

I decided to take my frustration and turn the apparel-printing hobby into something of a business. I kept receiving calls to make orders for schools and some small companies, which actually paid some of my bills and rent.

I had no idea what door this side hustle was going to open, but this decision changed my path in a major way.

THE BIRTH OF REFUTEES

DESIGNING AND PRINTING T-SHIRTS TO SELL AT THE
Portland Market on the weekends was my go-to hustle for
over a year. I knew most of the vendors from years prior
when I flipped gyros; now there I was with my own booth
and a different type of hustle than most of the Middle
Eastern community, who were still running all the food
booths.

The city of Portland was the basis for design inspiration.
I created a "Run Pdx" T-shirt with my friend Max and we
sold out all thirty-five T-shirts. It became a best-seller, and
I started making it in a variety of colors. We designed a
"Blazer" T-shirt with the basketball team's name written
vertically and the names of the players. We printed over
forty T-shirts and sold out the following week. I really
struggled at times, and went out a few weekends during
NBA Trail Blazers games in front of the stadium to sell

these T-shirts out of a duffle bag to make ends meet. The shirts sold, honestly not as well as I hoped. I had the courage to take those chances because it was survival mode—try anything with as few resources as were available.

A month later, I got a letter. It was my first cease and desist letter for copyright infringement for the Blazer shirt. I'd made roughly $1,500 from that shirt, but they wanted to put me in jail and fine me a ton of money. The NBA lawyer kept trying to get a hold of me, and I dodged his calls and letters. Finally, I found the courage and answered the phone. I explained how this was a misunderstanding and that I am not selling them anymore. He lowered my fine down from $5,600 to $3,500, and I agreed to pay it if he could give me some time.

He gave me until the end of the month, and it was already mid-July. The only thing I had of that value was the shop equipment. I decided this was it. I had to get out of this business. I found an eager buyer that week, and I sold everything to him for $8,000. I wrote a check to the NBA, mailed it out, feeling the weight come off. I barely survived with the money I had left, after paying for rent, food, and transportation.

I spent the next few months doing my best to get a job of any kind. My job search was going nowhere. I got very close to getting a job at Nike, one of the largest employers in the Portland and Beaverton area. I grew up so close to the headquarters, and we used to drive by and I would think to myself it would be so cool to work for Nike. Sadly, I couldn't communicate well enough and got rejected multiple times.

After months of searching, I opened a Hookah lounge with my brother Mohammed. Though the business took off and he went on to do well for a few years, it hurt our relationship early on and we had to go our separate ways. It was bittersweet to watch something I helped build flourish but not be a part of it. After four years, he sadly had to close it because he lacked the business acumen to keep it going further. However, something really good did come out of this experience. This is where I met Hannah, who I would later call my wife. The universe plays funny tricks. It's hard to see the silver lining during rough patches in life, but things happen for a particular reason.

I was out of work yet again in 2012 and needed to do something fast. If I restarted the print shop, I could earn some money. I knew everything I needed to make a T-shirt. I got some used equipment from Craigslist and found a space in downtown Beaverton. The rent was low, and the space was everything I needed.

For the next month, I spent days and nights setting up the shop. The production was basic, but I could print one-to-two hundred T-shirts per day and earn some cash. I started to feel the flow again. It was slow, but I had something. A purpose for getting up and doing creative work.

I realized my past mistakes had been teaching me all along. I focused and began to learn all about the screen-printing industry, going to seminars, reading books, taking classes, and watching tons of videos on YouTube to learn the tricks. I started getting orders from all kinds of community organizations, businesses, and schools. Some were small orders of ten T-shirts, and some were 300 garments or more.

I met two cool guys, Mark and Kimo, who worked at Nike. These two guys helped me build my business as they needed high-paying orders done quickly. They loved helping the little guy and wanted to see me succeed. They gave me a chance to play in the big leagues of printing. They started to consistently bring me work, as they needed T-shirts for all kinds of summer events. The work required a fast turnaround to ship out. I spent countless hours in the shop manually printing hundreds of garments.

I used some of the money I earned to invest in better equipment. I was always looking for ways to improve the printing process. As my business grew, I hired my brother Yas to help me with printing and other needs around the shop. He needed some part-time work and I needed part-time help; it was perfect. In 2014, we moved to the next town over to a warehouse space. By updating our website, redoing our name and branding, we started to attract more customers locally and nationally.

We named the business The Printory: Printing with Purpose. Our mission was to create unity through printed apparel. I wanted to go beyond earning a profit and give back.

For months, I wrestled with the idea to fill a shipping container with blankets, clothing, and shoes to ship to refugee camps. I visualized a container outside the shop that told a story. Throughout the year, people who visited could contribute or donate goods to fill it up.

I went to a TEDx Portland event to seek inspiration. I was fascinated by the talks. All of the ideas and stories that roamed the building were enlightening. After the show ended, I went outside and spotted Cody Goldberg, one of the speakers from the day. Cody had started a non-profit to build playgrounds with accessibility for all kids. His daughter's disability inspired him to develop and build playgrounds around Portland. I walked up and introduced myself and told him that I appreciated his work.

I asked if I could be of service to his company, and we exchanged numbers. The next week, he came to the shop and we talked about business and my personal story. I shared my idea to fill a shipping container full of goods and T-shirts to send to a refugee camp.

He paused and replied, "You mean like 'REFU-TEES'?"

I paused for a moment. "YES, exactly. That's what we can call it!"

I loved the sound of Ref-u-tees rolling off my tongue and started brewing ideas of what Refutees could be. I realized it shouldn't be a container to send across the world just yet. I needed to start somewhere smaller, starting with a box of garments that we would give away at the end of every quarter.

The first thing I did was align Refutees with prominent local organizations. IRCO and Catholic Charities had helped us so much when we first arrived in Portland in 1994. I decided to use my positive T-shirt graphics and create a series of Refutees to sell. It was time to shed light on the refugee crisis and provoke conversation for change.

After years of struggling with how screen-printing fit into my life, and the purpose of my business, the concept of Refutees pulled everything together.

WISDOM IN PAIN

———

ON NOVEMBER 30, 2016, I RECEIVED A PHONE CALL
that changed everything. My father, who had been visiting
Iraq for several months, died from a sudden heart attack.
I felt my life force pull out of me. It all seemed so unreal. I
was distraught and confused. I still needed time with him.

All my siblings came rushing over to my apartment to
comfort my mom. We all booked tickets to go to Iraq to
take care of our father's funeral. We arrived in our town of
As Samawah, and it was the first time the whole family was
back in Iraq together. My father was buried. In the Islamic
faith, the sooner someone is laid into the earth after they
pass, the better. I didn't get to see my father one last time.
I had to figure out another way to talk with him.

During the ceremony, the weight of it hit me. Traditionally,
the men in the family in our tribe stand in a line and greet

people, while people come to show respect and say a few prayers. But I couldn't stop thinking about the moments my father and I were together. They all came in a rush of emotion, and the only thing I could do was burst into tears.

The gathering brought over 3,000 people. People came from everywhere, as far as Baghdad. I had been to some funerals in the States at our local mosque, but they were never this big. The mosque was open for anyone who wanted to say a prayer and commune with those who were mourning.

My father had taken me to a couple of funerals when I visited Iraq a few years prior. When we went, he sat next to me, closed his eyes, and recited a Quranic Surah, usually Al Fatiha, The Opener. He repeated it a few times as he got more into his thoughts and prayer. I tried to repeat his steps that help calm and ease the mind.

"I'll be here one day; don't forget to pray for me," he had said. I didn't want to believe that my father would one day pass. He was always reminding me that time on earth is short. "Make sure you get the most out of it, never stop praying, treat yourself and others with respect."

He never stopped trying to teach me. Every opportunity was a teachable moment. I didn't realize how much he passed down to me. It's as if my life and his are one, and I can feel what he'd been trying to tell me throughout his life.

A part of me was angry, a part of me was confused, and a part of me accepted that Allah has the ultimate plan. My father's journey needed to end at this moment in time. I didn't want to accept this for weeks and months after. He was seventy-two years old, and his time came fast, where no one had a chance to embrace him one last time.

After Saddam Hussein was sentenced to death on December 30, 2006, for his crimes against humanity, many things began to change. My family began to frequently visit Iraq and build a new home in our city of Samawah. This home served as a revolving open door for all of us to visit when we wanted to reconnect with family and visit the holy cities and shrines in Karbala, Najaf, and Baghdad. My father loved visiting at least for a few weeks to a month every so often. These trips ensured his vision of returning and rebuilding our home. He created an art studio in one of the bedrooms and continued his life of painting and creating when he visited. His life, lived through a paintbrush, helped bring him all the way back where he once lived and roamed to help serve his community.

He was preparing for his morning prayer and passed before he could get on his prayer rug. In all reality, it's how he wanted to pass on. In his home country and his home.

The destiny was fulfilled; he knew he was going back home, he knew he was going to rebuild, he was the most patient.

My father passed, preparing for the one job he looked forward to every single day—his prayer.

This is how I came to understand the word "Inshallah" and how it manifests through a deep knowing that you return to where you belong. We are but visitors here on Earth.

After the funeral, my family and I spent three weeks in Iraq. I was afraid to go upstairs to his art room. I tried for a week, and each time I started crying when I entered. His art room was full of paintings, art supplies, and over a hundred paintings that he used for art shows. I finally gathered and wrapped them in plastic to store. All I could think about was one day making a gallery to showcase his remarkable artwork. I merely wanted to be with him and have one last conversation. I felt like I still had more to talk about than I ever had before.

My family was unsure where to go from this point; none of us had grieved like this before. Our love for him was strong, and we all felt a piece of ourselves missing. My mother struggled with it the most. His passing had changed something in all of us.

When I finally came back home to Portland, my taste for life had utterly changed.

I couldn't stop thinking about him. My mind was a mess,

and I started to buckle under all the pressures around me. Smiling was completely fake, and I was trying to run a business that I wasn't sure about anymore. My relationships with some people diminished. I was grieving, but I had no idea what that even meant. I simply realized that life is utterly short and that I had been spending my time on things that didn't necessarily matter; pleasing people and doing things that I didn't enjoy seemed absolutely absurd. Knowing that I, too, was headed to the same resting place as my father made every object, issue, and matter insignificant. Clarity was surfacing in the midst of my confusion.

The inner guiding compass led me to a place I had never been before—my own mortality. I stared down a deep well of my own pain and sorrow. This is the portal to the other side of this reality. The portal was a mirror that held up a unique reflection of what is, and what could be. I needed this time of reflection and deep thought. I needed to feel the pain and deepest emotion of letting go of someone I admired and loved. This portal is the entrance to the other side, the side my father had been telling me about my whole life. The only difference now is he was on the other side of the portal with a completed mission, and I was on this side, yet to complete my own.

LAYER 8

RELATIONSHIPS

WE ALL SAT AROUND A HUGE MOSQUE WHILE THE prayers from the Quran poured poetry over the people who came to my father's funeral ceremony in As Samawah, Iraq. People by the droves showed up during the afternoon hours. People stopped in to respect a man who led a beautiful family, and through art, charisma, and kindness, he spread one thing—love—to his community. With our heads down and tears running down our faces, I realized the phenomenal impact my father had on his community in Iraq.

The number of people who knew of him, the ones he would constantly call and check in with. The friends that were as far as the Art School of Baghdad and as near as our neighbors and immediate family. All were feeling the loss of a man who was a huge part of a connected community. I loved him even more for that. I loved that his essence lived on beyond his material body, the perfume that lingered in the minds of his friends, colleagues, family members, and me.

Relying on friendships, partnerships, and the relationship with ourselves is the most important work we can be involved with daily. Relationships are the core of everything we do. The value you bring is important, and the most important relationship we can establish and maintain is the one with our self, mind, and body.

Much like the layers that lay around this pivotal one. The connection layer tethers all of the ones around it and keeps them alive through constant communication and maintenance. Checking in with myself, staying actively aware of who I am in the act of staring into the mirror, and speaking to myself words of kindness and love. Checking in and reaching out to all of my supportive structures helps keep communication lines strong and healthy. Maintaining healthy connections and letting go of ones that hinder growth and unhealthy habits.

CONNECTION

———

THE PRINTORY STARTED AS A HOBBY, WHICH TURNED into a legitimate business printing multi-contract deals with local and national organizations. I didn't fully understand how to run my business, and I was constantly feeling growing pains. This once garage business had turned into something that consumed all my life, time, energy, and resources. I was climbing an uphill battle.

I wanted to serve my community with printed apparel to create unity in and around organizations, teams, schools, and small businesses. In return, I got tons of learning experiences and built relationships that I wouldn't trade for gold. The print shop was a vision to have a Willy Wonka type feel where students and people from all over came to visit and learn about the industry and the fun of printed apparel. This vision to a degree came to fruition; however, without the proper team I couldn't get it to fully realize.

From this work, I was able to sink deep into community involvement and built a massive network that helped me in more ways than I can count.

When Refutees was born inside the print shop, it began to heal a wound of my past trauma and began to give voice through powerful messaging. The two businesses are difficult to manage and maintain together. Refutees is a way to spread awareness and has a retail aspect of needing constant attention. I wanted to create a very unique design aesthetic around powerful messages, create unique releases, and focus on community-building around our cause of giving back needed products to the local refugee community. After months of efforts, marketing, and pushing the concept to friends, family, and our social media audience, Refutees began to garner attention.

The work, however, was a constant battle to keep it alive and maintain the bulk printing side of the business at The Printory. Managing people, clients, community engagements, and an endless array of emails and scheduling with low capital, was extremely difficult. My mounting pressure and belief that I could do it all was hindering growth on all fronts.

After my father's passing, I realized the clear-cutting I needed to take care of to get things where they needed to be, working for me while I focused on doing what I actually love doing.

I decided the time had come to trim anything that wasn't healthy in my life. I dug deeper into my habits to fix myself, one thing at a time. I downsized the shop back into one unit, sold an embroidery machine, and started to get my financials back in order. Selling the entire shop was not too far off in the distance, but I began slowly slicing off chunks so that I could manage this transition. I let go of clients that were always giving us a hard time, and some employees, too. I reduced everyone's hours. I tried to be as frugal as I could as I slashed expenses. I wanted to rid myself of any excess that I couldn't or didn't want to manage anymore. I was getting over the shock of my father's death and beginning to process it all. My pain began to turn into wisdom.

This was a transformational focus on repairing a lost relationship with myself. I was so much for everyone around me, but I barely took care of myself. I didn't eat with proper nutrition, and I hardly exercised no matter how much I wanted to. My habits were so centered on managing the businesses that I had none for myself. I talked a lot and shared my story, but I never gave myself a chance to listen to my inner calm. I ignored so many red flags and gut feelings that were trying so hard to steer me in the right direction.

I struggled financially, and it seemed I couldn't earn enough to keep everything afloat. I tried very hard to get some loans to hire people to help me but was constantly denied. I felt alone on my journey. Though I had support and amazing people around me, I was too prideful to ask for serious help. This was a tough time for me, trying not to take it personally and keeping my deepest feelings apart from day-to-day activities. Smiling was becoming increasingly difficult.

I drowned out my inner guiding compass and covered my layers of resilience with blame, envy, and jealousy of those around me who I saw garnering the success that I longed for from a financial and business perspective. Financial perspective is just one of the hundreds of other lenses I could use to view the world. I kept telling myself that I was too busy to actually sit and listen to where my inner compass was trying to guide me.

Happiness, I realized, is a state of mind. My mindset relied on how I chose to place my energy, which was bound to my time. My time became the most valuable thing in the universe and where I was choosing to spend it was not on being envious, but rather replacing it to be more supportive and generous. Time spent serving was less time spent in negative and dark spaces of the mind.

"Hussein, Habibi, no one in the world can tell you where you need to go or how you should go about living your life. That's up to you to decide. Once you face your fears, the outer voices will diminish." My father's voice would come in and out of my thoughts as I moved with more intention to fix, heal, and rebuild myself from within.

I sacrificed all that didn't serve me to the gods of simplicity, calm, and peace. I drove out to the Oregon coast to clear my mind and go deep within myself at the beach. I had a full-blown conversation with my inner thoughts. I yelled at the top of my lungs, I tried to let it all out and let go and let myself feel the pain of loss pass through me.

At the beach, I looked out into the ocean and onto the horizon. I felt a calming silence. I realized this was my reset space. Where the sand meets water was where I could come to regain perspective. The infinite horizon of the ocean reassured me that I no longer needed to feel the scarcity of not only water but love and how much I am truly surrounded by it. I needed this moment of clarity to feel the abundance again.

The waves drowned out my thoughts. I sat in the sand in front of the water for hours, staring at the infinity of everything. I let go. I forgave every person that I believed wronged me in any way. They didn't ultimately matter in the plans ahead. I let go and forgave myself for my past mistakes; they led me here and I would rather have had those experiences than not. Every mistake taught me something valuable for my journey, and I had a long path to a healthy mind. The journey officially began to be worth it. I was in unity with myself, and I knew it then.

A MOMENT OF HAPPINESS

—

I WAS MAKING LEAPS AND BOUNDS IN REGAINING MY courage. I knew that being decisive was a monumental lesson, and I couldn't wait to make the most critical decision of my life: choosing my partner to live out this incredible journey with. A month after my trip to the beach, I knew it was time to make my connection to Hannah, my girlfriend, even deeper. I took her to the same beach, where we strolled, talked, and finally sat on the sand and watched the sunset. The clouds created a painting like a sunset for us to be in awe of Allah's beauty in the moment.

I waited for a few moments and let the waves of the ocean consume our deep thoughts and give us the calm we both longed for. I slowly reached in my pocket and pulled out a small rolled-up canvas sheet on which I had printed a Rumi poem called "A Moment of Happiness" and gave it to her to read.

A moment of happiness,
you and I sitting on the verandah,
Apparently two, but one in soul, you and I.
We feel the flowing water of life here,
you and I, with the garden's beauty
and the birds singing.
The stars will be watching us, and we will show them
What it is to be a thin crescent moon.
You and I unselfed, will be together,
indifferent to idle speculation, you and I.
In one form upon this Earth,
and in another form in a timeless sweet land.

Inside was a wedding ring that her grandmother wore. We loved one another and watched the sunset in a moment of happiness that has continued to last. We were both ready for the life in front of us. We got married in August of 2018. The celebration was a beautiful blend of Middle Eastern and Indian culture. Our families connected, danced, and ate delicious food together. The laughs, smiles, and love amplified our unity through the room. Our bond was official; our unity set the course for the beautiful life we intended to build.

With Hannah, I was more myself than I had ever been with anyone. I was more introspective and found it easier to better my habits and rid myself of my past lifeways. She had helped me through so much of the healing process—to forgive myself for the past mistakes, get on my feet, and spark my creativity back up again. I needed a teammate, a partner to trust my intuition to freely come out and speak to me. I can only hope that I bring to her what she brings to me.

Hannah and I teamed up in ways we didn't realize we could. We leaned into Refutees and started to get creative. The business and the products became a social justice vehicle to promote thought-provoking ideas. Our partnership began to foster and grow and lean into one another's strengths and weaknesses.

Our journeys are intertwined in faith, love, communication, belief in one another, and care for each other. Our immigrant and refugee backgrounds give us a more profound purpose. We share commonalities of heritage and depth of respect for our ancestors.

THE MESSAGE

—

WE'RE ALL FROM SOMEWHERE. THE REFUTEES MOTTO is a powerful reminder that we are all connected, and we are all from Earth. We all come from unique places and have differences, but that's what makes us all interesting. Drop knowledge—not bombs, Be Better, Peaceful state of mind, unity, are all messages woven with graphics that pull people in to provoke conversations.

These are all messages connected to resilience, art, and a way to spread a positive reminder. The T-shirt has been my canvas to speak louder for me. Whether I was at work, the gym, or walking around Portland, whenever I wore a Refutee, I always got asked, "Where did you get your T-shirt?" "I love the message!" or "What does your T-shirt say?" I get messages and emails daily about the compliments and conversations our T-shirts spark around the world. One peaceful conversation after another is precisely how Hannah and I want to spread our messages through Refutees.

Hannah and I bought a 1985 Volkswagen Vanagon that we cleaned up and made into our Refutee Mobile, where we do pop-ups all over Portland, Oregon. We use the van to carry around our merchandise but also to share our experience and build awareness. When I was at the refugee camp, VW Vanagons used to come around to toss toys and candy to kids during Eid, the holiday celebrated twice a year, after Ramadan and after the pilgrimage to Mecca. We made the Refutee Mobile a part of our experience to further tell my refugee story and create a deeper relationship to our cause. Our tribe of friends that we have been cultivating loved it. We made a fan and a friend everywhere we went.

I used to play with a lot of paper airplanes in the refugee camp. One day, the kids at the school made hundreds of paper airplanes and tossed them around. The white paper planes were everywhere, and I jumped in on the fun. It was one of the best days I remember from Refugee School. Now we fold our unique flyer that tells our whole story into paper airplanes. Everything in our booth and our work ties back to supporting refugees and sharing our story to build a meaningful tribal connection.

Being from a tribe is not the same as building a tribe of

people who love our work. This is not easy work; it takes a ton of courage to lead from within a message that can resonate around a mission. Our mission to spread awareness for refugees is one I'm continually bringing all of my layers of resilience to. This is the work that matters to me and who I am as a person. Refutees helped me in the healing process of past trauma. Leaning into that process has helped me clarify my mission and allow my inner compass to take over throughout the challenging times.

Our Refutees journey came to a head-on collision with COVID-19. The first few weeks shook everyone. The unknown is a wild and scary place. This moment is a lesson to lean into the many layers of resilience I have built up over the years. I've made it through some crazy life situations, but this time, I'm wiser. I can adapt faster, sit, and breathe through it. The days seem dark, but I can count off a million things I'm grateful for: running water, the roof over my head, food in the pantry. I know I have help if I need it as well.

During quarantine, I started painting again. It has been therapy to cope with everything happening. I've learned to pour my energy and time into something creative. I forgot how soothing and calming the painting was to my soul. Over four months, I painted a portrait of my father. I reconnected with him during the process. I understand now, more than ever, what he was doing late at night in the refugee camp.

The time away from the shop and the pause from the rat race feels good. When the Printory business started to suffer immediately after COVID hit, I had to adapt quickly. The time had come to make my final peace and sacrifice and sell the whole shop's equipment and warehouse space. An excruciating removal of many band-aids I had placed from the years prior. I pulled them all off fast and made a plan to sell the shop equipment and outsource the printing to another local print shop. This brokering opportunity relieved me of all my shop duties to focus on the projects I wanted to lean into. I have been building towards this for a few years, and the time came to step into the next phase of life.

Painting became a nightly ritual to continue a meditative practice to simply take it all in, stay out of the news and focus on healthy habits. I painted a man's image, almost a self-image wearing a red mask with the word "unity" across. Who would have thought that a mask would be the flag of the world? The painting archives this moment in time; it gives me fulfillment to reflect and create. I made the painting into a T-shirt, with "unity" written in a clean, simple font slanted upwards. The "i" was a stem and rose, a nod to Portland, the city of roses, and the uprising for Black Lives Matter protests.

The "Unity Rose" became an instant Refutees classic and the most successful T-shirt we had ever launched. We decided to donate the proceeds to Self Enhancement, Inc., a non-profit that helps young black youth get to college and does extraordinary after-school programs. Within hours, we sold hundreds of Unity T-shirts and donated thousands of dollars.

This painting turned into a T-shirt amplified everything I have been trying to say for the past ten years. Now that I have this focus, the tribe began to multiply with people seeking to support us even more.

CONCLUSION

KNOWLEDGE IS GOLDEN

It's late in the afternoon, and my father has dropped in on me at my print shop. He often comes to hang out and paints his canvases while I print T-shirts. He shares stories of art shows, people he's met before, and the places he has visited. He dips his paintbrush in oil paint and moves it across the canvas with precision, creating Arabic letters.

The canvas reads "Surat Al Fatiha," The Opener from the Quran. It is decorated with a floral Arabesque pattern and roses flowing through words. It is the prayer he and my mom kept reciting that very dark night of the Gulf War where he prayed over our lives. I watch as he fills the colors in, and he watches me as I screen print my art onto T-shirts. He talked about the Golden Era of Islam and the importance of knowledge, always asking what I'm reading and how it's helping me. My father's favorite way to express beauty and unity has been through roses, peace doves, and words and patterns that express joy.

While he helps me fold shirts, I talk a lot. He notices me often stop what I'm doing to make hand gestures. Impatient with my lack of work, he says, "Work with your hands, speak with your mouth. Make your actions louder than your words." It was my constant reminder to speak less, take action and let that speak for me. That painting of The Opener is the first thing I see when I walk into our home today. It's a reminder of my father and a reminder to believe in something greater than myself.

The Golden age of Islam was about expanding knowledge, reading, and translating works from every part of the ancient world. Knowledge and learning were at the epicenter of Baghdad at the House of Wisdom. Scholars from all over the ancient world roamed Iraq, building, creating, inventing, translating, and exporting knowledge and stories. The term "knowledge is golden" comes from this era. The rulers of the time offered the weight of a book in exchange for its weight in gold. Anyone who could bring forth unknown knowledge, further explore ideas, and build upon them could add a book to The House of Wisdoms Library.

Prophet Mohammed (peace be upon him) expressed the importance of this life-long search. "Seek knowledge from the cradle to the grave, even unto China." Knowledge is a lived experience further to understand oneself and the world around him or her. Knowledge is the fuel for action to do just about anything. Having an open mind can improve the way I see your world, with more understanding, love, and peace.

Having knowledge about myself and continuing to grow is the essence of the Refugee State of Mind. I'm no longer a refugee, but I seek refuge in my innermost deep thoughts. Here is where my mental fortitude lies. The structures, stories, experiences, and knowledge that hold up the layers of resilience create a healthy mindset that can weather all conditions. A reminder that the unfortunate situation of living in a camp was my training ground, the mental gym I needed to build the pathways for transformation. It prepared me for my journey to America, where I could grow and prosper. I needed every ounce of that experience to become who I am today. This is why I embrace my refugee experience, though it is not one I would wish on anyone.

The morning that my family woke up after the bombing of our city was a gift. It was my opportunity to pursue life. From that day forward, everything changed. We moved to America, and I tried to change my clothes, shoes, haircut, language, and cultural norms and even considered changing my name. Change on the exterior is very temporary, and it rarely ever lasts.

When I was uncomfortable with my name, my father taught me why he named me Hussein. Imam Hussein, son of Imam Ali and the Prophet Mohammed's grandson. Imam Hussein stood and sacrificed himself for truth, love, compassion, equality, and knowledge. He told me my name is a reminder to apply those teachings to my life. I get to carry the name of a leader, who exemplified profound courage and was an example to follow to be the better version of myself.

* * *

Internal change is not easy. The challenges of growth are always going to be the forces that push against me. These forces helped me build layers of resilience, and they will help you, too.

You have so much power inside you already; knowing it is half the battle. By now, you may have seen some of your life and story woven with some of my experiences. However, your family may have come here years ago. They may have been immigrants from Europe, Asia, Africa, South America, or even more remote islands. They may have been refugees fleeing for safety and escaping the wrath of a warlord or a dictator.

We're all from somewhere, specifically this magnificent spaceship called Earth; no one land belongs to one person. It is our collective responsibility to take care of the Earth and each other.

Resilience is part of who we all are as humans; we have it deep within us. I hope this story has brought you closer to understanding your art, story, creativity, and layers of resilience. Power to the peaceful.

Refugees, immigrants, and other marginalized groups add so much richness to our culture. Telling stories and sharing conversations about resilience is a powerful way to create more unity. Resilience is a critical thread that weaves itself into the fabric of our collective human story.

Spreading awareness about refugees may help end wars and reduce hate crimes or lead to peace talks and new ideas on how to solve old problems. Without awareness and speaking up, how will our voices be heard? To raise awareness is to create understanding.

We cannot wait for others to swoop in and help. We must do our part. We can be the spark that helps light the path for someone in the darkness. I may not change the world, but I hope to inspire someone who can keep paving the long path ahead, just as my ancestors did for me. While my father taught me to rise and create, my brother painted "Power to the Rebels" on schools' walls. I write "Power to the Peaceful" across posters and garments to help empower and spread awareness. We must rise to create a better self, and in turn, make a better community. My guiding compass leads me through very challenging times to unfold my mission so that I may appreciate all that will come from my deep understanding.

Creating graphics and art comes to me in waves from everything around me, and I try to trust my instinct as soon as a concept comes to mind. As I was thinking of the Art of Resilience mission, I wanted a metaphoric graphic I could use across all media.

The resilience rose graphic began as a sketch to explore how the Art of Resilience mission would come to life. I almost didn't share it with my publisher's graphics team; fear of judgment played a role. I had to share it, and I'm glad I did. They helped me develop the idea into an iconic graphic that will withstand the test of time.

A rose represents an offering of a peaceful solution, a way to create a bridge and celebrate our human connection. The fist brings together empowerment, a nod to all who have raised a fist against all forms of injustice. It is a symbol for those who stand for human equality, equity, justice, and peace. This graphic is the emblem of work ahead. It will resonate as the icon of resilience for all who lead the peaceful way.

I received the Portland Home Town Hero Award in March of 2021 for our work with Refutees and the community engagement for the past eight years. After being fined by the NBA, I never thought this circle would loop in this way.

Never giving up on who you actually want to become is the truest form of reward. I merely wanted to use my art for a side hustle and pay my rent and make sure I had gas money by selling those T-shirts. I was trying my best and doing whatever it took to make an extra couple of dollars. Standing on the Rose Garden, now named Moda Center Stadium, corner in the rain all those years ago with a duffle bag full of T-shirts. I'm grateful for the reconnection, but I'm even more grateful that I took the chance on myself.

I had no idea that I would get fined and potentially go to jail. I risked my freedom without even knowing it for artistic expression—something in my bloodline, I suppose, risking freedom for art. Never giving up means constant accountability for self and ensuring growth happens through consistent practice. I'm excited to turn these opportunities into more awareness vehicles for the refugee community.

My internal guiding compass keeps nudging me to continue to the next mission. The Refutees Mobile became a parked, useless storage van during the COVID pandemic. I wanted to ensure we could use it to explore my next mission. I reached out to Portland State University and asked for sponsorship to develop my next idea. With my friends' help, we were able to transform the interior into a mobile podcast studio. Stories need to be told from every lens. Resilience lives in all of us, and this is the vehicle to bring those stories to life. I created The Art of Resilience Podcast show to invite people to share their immigrant and refugee stories, businesses, community organizing, and policy work to show just how resilience plays into the lives of all humans.

THE RESILIENCE CLUB

Most of us leave the important work—like writing a book, painting, starting a business, filming a documentary—to chance that "we will get to it later." This is resistance, a deep well that draws buckets of fear to feed you the concept that you are not good enough to pursue that mission. It comes up in all types of forms; it could be something as subtle as "I have to do the dishes before I start." How about one more episode before I start? Sadly, "later" turns into weeks, months, and years of our lives. We blame and flip to the dark side of envy, jealousy, resentment, anger, and frustration.

Please don't go to the dark side. I have been there, and it is a horrible place to live in our minds. The choice is ours. We only need to do one thing and hold ourselves accountable to show up for ourselves.

The only way we improve at absolutely anything is to practice it as often as we possibly can. This is why prayer was so essential to my father's teaching of self-mastery. Prayer wasn't just about religion, faith, or even asking for something. It was a habit to practice gratitude to live in the moment. If I can bring myself to the prayer rug three times per day, I can do just about anything. He held himself accountable, which is the deep well from which all of our resilience draws buckets of energy.

I want to continue this story and conversation, and I have built an action-based accountability group that can help us focus. The Resilience Club is an online space to meet up and to create something extraordinary together to amplify our work to serve.

We meet to create and build an essential habit of prioritizing ourselves and dreams of taking on our own missions. We share wins, ideas, love, and virtual high fives. We share an endless array of resources to help one another overcome fear and self-doubt.

This is a supportive environment for all to learn from one another and become better through practice. I encourage you to join, listen in, and start a habit to put you and your dreams first. This is a positivity-oriented group, so be aware, smiles, laughter, and joy are to be had to the fullest.

All my experiences seem to have a pattern of loops that exemplify how one day those experiences return to serve me somehow. I may not know how it will unfold, but I can trust my inner layers of resilience that it's all for the good of my lived human experience.

You can join The Resilience Club and uncover your resilience layers to catapult yourself and work to the next oasis of knowledge. I invite you to watch or listen to The Art of Resilience Podcast at husseinalbaiaty.com. If you or someone you know wants to be involved in our podcast to help sponsor or further amplify our work, please send us an email through husseinalbaiaty.com.

Has my story inspired you? Has it moved you to take action in some way? The easiest way to help spread this work and message is to share it with someone who needs to hear my story. You are a part of my journey, and I hope to be a part of yours. I cannot climb this path without your help. I'm asking you to spread my message, so everyone may develop a unique state of mind of their own to face their challenges. I'm of service to you, your organization, your team, classroom, school, and community.

I would love to hear from you and hear about your own journey. Please don't hesitate to reach out to me through our website husseinalbaiaty.com.

Salam, my brothers and sisters. May Allah help us recognize our strengths and the beauty in unity. Seek knowledge and spread peace.

ACKNOWLEDGMENTS

THANK YOU TO MY SOULMATE, PARTNER, AND THE reason I have grown to understand what love can be. You are the ocean to the beach I walk on, for I am in awe by the abundance of love you share. Hannah, I'm grateful for your unwavering belief in who I am. Your continued effort to nourish, heal, and grow through understanding and patience is something I pray to Allah I never lose. Thank you for fueling my creative confidence to complete this book and pursue our dreams, art, and life together.

To the sun and the moon of my universe. My mother, Jassmia, and father, Kamel. You have given me more than I can ever fathom, and I'm humbled by the faith in which you passed down. To my remarkable siblings Alaa, Yas, Zainab, Ozzie, Mohammed, and Heba. You are all the stars that give the night sky beauty. Thank you all for being the support structures I needed in all aspects of life. I'm grateful for all that you have sacrificed to ensure I reach my full potential. I cannot imagine life without all of your love.

To my extended family, teachers, mentors, and inner circle of friends. You are all the resilient plants in the garden I love to tend. Thank you for opening your doors, welcoming me, and expanding my mind and experiences. Thank you for believing in my talents, nourishing me and supporting me when I lacked belief in them myself. I have a broader lens to see, love, and appreciate the world because of all of you.

To all whom I have known, met briefly, and even lost touch. You are all pieces of gold in my memory bank. Thank you for coming on to the show of my life. I rely on your imparting wisdom, lessons, sharing meals, ideas, empowerment, coffee, laughs, arguments, and debates. You have strengthened me and added value to who I am, and I'm grateful for you all.

To the great staff at Scribe Media. Thank you for helping me bring my story out of my mind, body, and soul and transform it into this book for the world.

May Allah continue to bless you all with health and keep you all for your loved ones. As-salamu alaikum.

CPSIA information can be obtained
at www.ICGtesting.com
Printed in the USA
JSHW031958140621
15906JS00001B/9